GW00546684

Contents

Introduction

The twentieth century has brought about many changes and as we enter the twenty-first century our lives continue to be transformed. In some ways the world seems smaller. We can use the internet to link us to individuals anywhere in the world, within hours we can travel across the world and even explore space! In other ways, the planet earth seems to be growing rapidly. The world population continues to grow and as a result cities are expanding and more are being built and transport facilities are having to accommodate the increasing numbers.

In many ways, our world seems to be a better place. Scientific and medical advances continue to make our lives more comfortable, in some countries there is greater equality between men and women, and governments are accepting greater responsibility for the welfare of their citizens. Yet, in other ways the twentieth century has brought many problems. Despite all the wonderful advances we have witnessed throughout the century most people agree that the world and its future faces threat. Almost on a daily basis the mass media reports on some of the biggest issues of our time. We are subjected to images of the innocent victims of war or violence, the poor or unemployed struggling to survive, young people huddled together in doorways and clear evidence of the threat to the environment. All these terrible images should bring home the message that the planet and the human race face enormous problems.

What issues do you find the most worrying and the most interesting? A simple question you might think. Yet, if you ask a group of people to make a list of the ten issues that worry and interest them, you would be almost bound to get totally different answers. Clearly no textbook can cover all the issues

which should be of concern to us today. The *A–Z of PSE* asks some hard questions, comprehensively dealing with the subject matter in a variety of new and challenging ways. It attempts to raise your awareness of some of these important topics by giving you relevant, up-to-date information, leaving you to draw your own conclusions. It is hoped that, as you read about the topics explored in this book, you will be able to understand them better and begin to develop and express your own views.

The book is divided into 26 individual units covered by the letters A to Z. Each unit has a single word title for ease of reference – Addiction, Celebrity, Environment, Violence, etc. Each unit is set in context with a specific aim, definition, and notable quotations, enabling you to see what areas you will be covering. All of the units contain stimulus material including photographs, diagrams, cartoons and activities designed to promote reflection, discussion and the opportunity for you to increase your knowledge of the topic.

The discussion activities are designed to promote debate on PSHE issues either for the whole class, small groups or pair work. You may be asked to note down the main points of discussion, feed back your ideas to the rest of the class or engage in role-play situations. In this way, it is hoped that your understanding of the topic will deepen and critical, evaluative and empathy skills will be developed. The written activities are designed to encourage you to develop your ability to interpret and understand information, and then to respond to them using your own thoughts and ideas.

Certain words or key terms are highlighted in blue throughout the text where they first appear. These are defined or explained in more detail in a separate glossary at the end of this title.

Addiction

Every form of addiction is bad.
(Carl Gustav Jung, Psychologist)

Addiction: used to describe the state of people who are taken over by something which once helped them or gave them pleasure.

In a consumer society there are inevitably two kinds of slave: the prisoners of addiction and the prisoners of envy.
(Ivan Illich, Philosopher)

AIM The unit examines different types of addiction and the reasons why some people repeat behaviour, even though they know the harm and dangers their addiction is causing to themselves and others.

Until recently 'addiction' has usually been associated with the illegal taking of drugs or the more socially acceptable use of alcohol and tobacco. Some addictions are fairly harmless: others can become compulsive and destructive. Addicts often know they are doing themselves harm, but just cannot stop.

In today's society addiction means we have to look at a number of different areas. Addicts are not necessarily people who take drugs, smoke or drink. Anything which a person feels unable to stop easily can be described as an 'addiction'.

Some substances such as drugs and alcohol can cause a physical dependence, therefore, if a person stops taking them they may suffer withdrawal symptoms. Other addictions, such as gambling, are caused by a psychological dependence where the individual feels good.

Experts believe that addiction could happen to anyone of any age or social status. Young people, in particular, are vulnerable to trends and persuasive advertising. In the late 1990s newspaper headlines often referred to the 'fashion junkies' who were addicted to designer clothes and even designer bodies. Being told how to look and feel costs the addict not just their money but, in some cases, their entire personality.

A Different types of addiction

Activity

1 Look at figure **A** and draw a chart with two columns, one headed '**physical**' and the other '**psychological**'. Try and place each addiction under the heading which you think is the most appropriate. Think of as many addictions as you can and list them in the correct column.

IN THE NEWS

DRUG ABUSE 'NOT OUT OF CONTROL'

TV shopping channels create addicts

MAN SELLS CAR IN ORDER TO BUY LOTTERY TICKETS

ADDICTED TO POWER

Supermodels responsible for slimming addiction craze

1 The headlines cover many addictions. Most addictions make the person's life a misery but some can cause thousands of other people to suffer. In groups, decide which headline highlights an addiction causing suffering on a large scale. Select one member of your group to report your views to the rest of the class.

Addicts often argue that they should not be stopped or punished for doing something which harms them and no one else. The problem with this seemingly logical argument is that it is flawed. Without doubt drug and alcohol addictions are very destructive and contribute to the increasing crime rates, particularly amongst young people. An addiction to a substance such as tobacco can affect others through passive smoking, and gambling has ruined the lives of many families financially and emotionally.

Like other forms of addiction, the compulsive gambler finds that he/she needs more and more of the 'drug'. The excitement becomes dependent on the size of the risk being taken. There appears to be four main 'attractions' for the gambler:

1 The dream of instant riches is very strong for people brought up in a society where money and wealth are regarded as important. Winning the football pools or the National Lottery gives everyone the chance to have access to 'instant' wealth.

2 It helps to counteract boredom and loneliness. People love the risks and excitement of the instant pay-outs on scratch cards or fruit machines.

3 We believe that we cannot lose all the time and that, if we keep trying long enough, eventually we will beat the system. Despite the incredibly long odds of winning the jackpot in the National Lottery people are still prepared to spend some of their money on tickets.

4 Many of us believe that money is the answer to long term security. The media like stories of people whose lives have improved after a huge financial win, but we prefer to ignore those stories about people whose lives have fallen apart after receiving massive sums of money.

THINK ABOUT

1 *Do you agree with the following views?*

'It's only a bit of fun. It's exciting and no one gets hurt.'

'It's a way of getting something for nothing.'

'Gambling does more harm than good.'

2 *Look at the four 'attractions' for the gambler. What other reasons can you suggest for why people gamble? Who do you think are the most vulnerable members of society? What do you think is the great attraction of gambling for so many young people?*

Alcohol remains Britain's main problem drug and evidence proves it is linked to a large number of violent crimes and driving offences. Drinking alcohol is seen by many as socially acceptable and some medical experts actually think that a small amount is good for you. The media often contributes to this 'healthy image' just as in the past it helped to promote smoking as a relaxing activity.

The problems come for those individuals who drink too much, become dependent on (addicted to) alcohol or whose drinking causes problems for those around them. Unfortunately, the physical and mental health of a person is increasingly affected the more they drink.

B   Images in the media: John Travolta in *Pulp Fiction*

Smoking also used to be socially acceptable. It was fashionable amongst the rich and famous and smokers were often regarded as intelligent, more mature and 'macho'. Film stars in the 1930s to 1950s helped to contribute to this 'image building'. In the 1990s however, health groups have repeatedly objected to the fact that although smoking is banned in most cinemas, scenes of film stars lighting up cigarettes are increasing.

Today we are much more aware of the health risks of smoking and the fact that it causes thousands of premature deaths. Even inhaling other people's cigarette smoke (passive smoking) can increase the risk of lung cancer. Despite the proven dangers of smoking and restrictions on cigarette advertising there are concerns that smoking is yet again becoming popular, especially amongst young people.

Activities

2   You have been out with a group and the person who is driving you home has been drinking. One of your friends refuses to accept the lift home and the others try and persuade him/her otherwise. Role-play the scene, with different people acting the role of the person refusing the lift.

3   Is it easy to resist the pressure from the rest of the group and say no? What arguments were used?

Why do people smoke?   c

Pleasure

Relaxation

Peer pressure

Image

HABIT

Activities

4 Why do you think some people drink to excess?
What do you think of the following people who
get very drunk:
a) teenage boys;
b) teenage girls;
c) adults?

5 Every cigarette packet carries a government
health warning. Yet despite this, people still
smoke. Some surgeons have refused to carry out
operations unless the patient agrees to give up
smoking. Do you think they are right? Give
reasons for your answer.

6 Should smoking be banned in all public places?
Give reasons for your answer.

7 Select some of the information in this unit and
use it in a poster or advert designed to warn
young people of the dangers of
addictions.

Fortunately there is hope for people with
addictions: an addiction is not something
fixed that can never be altered. Admittedly
some addictions are much more difficult to
deal with than others and we still do not
know why some people develop them.
Therapy, support, counselling, and
treatment can provide hope but the real
problem is that the addict must face up to
their problem and be ready to ask for help.

What do you think ?

*With the knowledge we have and
knowing the dangers, why do you
think people still become 'victims
of addiction'?*

Body

The more imperfect we feel, the more we strive for some image of being perfect.

(Susie Orbach, Author)

Body: the physical structure of a person

We should look to the mind, and not to the outward appearances.

(Aesop, Writer of fables)

AIM The unit examines the positive and negative 'body images' that are promoted by the fashion and beauty industries and presented by the media.

In recent years there has been increasing criticism of the multi-million pound fashion and beauty industries. In order to promote their goods they make use of models who 'strike the pose' and present a particular image to a target audience. In spite of the best efforts of campaigners many believe that beauty magazines still carry advertisements which present unrealistic images. The 'perfect body' is emphasised and young women in particular are targeted for the 'hard sell'; nowadays the media have begun to sell this ideal to young men as well.

IN THE NEWS

No fun being female

Cosmetic surgery – now men want it as well!

Can boys be anorexic?

CHANGING THE ATTITUDES OF MILLIONS

Time the fashion world got real!

1 In pairs look at the five headlines and try to explain what you think each one is about. What is the story behind each headline?

2 In groups discuss how powerful body images are in the media. Try to give examples. Do you think the obsession for the perfect body is good?

A   The images that influence and sell

We live in a culture which is dominated by television, video, magazines and advertising. Time and time again, the fashion world is criticised for using images in the media where poverty and sexual conflict are exhibited and exploited.

Today the media dictate what is and is not beautiful. People have never been under so much pressure to conform to particular images and not everyone can or wants to. Some fashion houses use **waif-like** models and young children to promote their goods. In the late 1990s, one fashion trend was condemned for using photos of hollow-eyed, wasted models with 'heroin chic', the features normally associated with heroin addicts.

For years parents have complained that magazines tempt their children, usually girls, to develop eating disorders and use drugs. As a result, fashion magazines often carry problem pages as well as glossy adverts.

The obsession with perfection has created thousands of 'victims'. In America there is a trend of parents entering their very young children for pageantry or beauty contests. Children as young as five years-old are dressed up to look and perform as adults. In some cases the parents even pay for cosmetic surgery to make minor changes to their child's appearance.

Activity

1   In pairs role-play a scene where one person is a fashion critic insisting that the fashion items in figure **A** are indecent. The other person is the fashion designer trying to justify their creations.

Imagery – tasteful or obscene?   **B**

THINK ABOUT

1 Discuss the following statements and decide whether you agree or disagree with them:

People are far too worried about their physical appearance.

People look at the whole you, not just one individual part.

You can always find a fault in anyone's appearance. No one has the body they would have chosen.

Choose someone to note down your group's conclusions and feedback to the rest of the class.

In the past, plastic or reconstructive surgery was offered for people disfigured by accidents, birth defects or certain operations, such as breast cancer. Today many operations take place for cosmetic purposes, mainly to improve appearance in an otherwise generally healthy person.

In Britain it is estimated that over 65,000 people a year have cosmetic surgery, many of them for breast enlargement. Some women want silicone breast implants (**C**) because they think their new figure will bring them success, increased confidence and attractiveness in a male orientated world. The request for an operation suggests that the woman feels inadequate about her appearance. Although it is usually claimed that these implants do not interfere with natural breastfeeding, this is not the case as milk ducts or glandular tissue can be affected. There are increasing numbers of legal cases being brought against the manufacturers of the implants which some women believe have caused them medical problems. Some people feel that women who have small breasts are somehow seen as less attractive. Breast size does not denote attractiveness: in the 1920s, the 1960s and the early 1990s to be flat-chested was the 'in thing'.

The popular view is that obsession with 'perfection' comes mainly from women, however, increasing numbers of men are also requesting surgery in the search of the 'perfect body'.

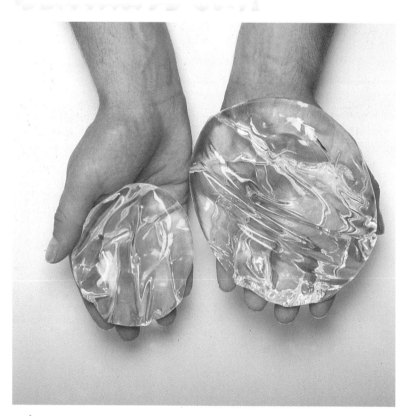

C Silicone implants – the 'perfect' body?

Another consequence of this obsession for perfection is the increasing number of people suffering from food disorders. Bulimia and anorexia are most common among girls and young women and in Britain 6,000 new sufferers are registered annually. It is a fact that the only time since 1935 that the anorexia rate has dipped was in the 1950s, when the two most famous female film stars were Marilyn Monroe and Jayne Mansfield (**D**). Both had a fuller figure and this was regarded as the fashionable shape for women.

A major concern is the rise in eating disorders among children. A woman is diagnosed as suffering from anorexia nervosa if her weight is 15% below normal and she has not had a period for three months. Anorexia is the most serious eating disorder because it can be fatal: 10% of anorexics die from their illness. Bulimia nervosa is a newly recognised condition where an individual has two or more binge-eating periods (rapid consumption of large amounts of food – even frozen or raw) each week for at least three months. These binges are followed by vomiting or the misuse of **laxatives**.

Activities

2 What is the difference between plastic and cosmetic surgery?

3 To what extent is the mass media responsible for marketing the 'perfect body'?

4 Why is there so much pressure in modern Western society to be slim and good looking?

5 How much do you know about eating disorders? Answer true or false to the following statements:

a) Anorexics never think about food.
b) Young men are less likely to suffer from anorexia than young women.
c) Crash diets are a good way to lose weight.
d) Eating disorders are a problem in all countries of the world.
e) During a binge, a bulimic might eat food that is raw or frozen.
f) If a woman loses too much weight her menstrual cycle is affected.
g) We only eat when we are hungry.

1950s – Jayne Mansfield (above)
1990s – Jodie Kidd (below)

D

Two new conditions are now appearing: binge-eating disorder is where someone binges like a bulimic but does not make him/herself sick or use laxatives afterwards. Prader-Willi syndrome is much more rare. It is a genetic disorder with symptoms of an uncontrollable appetite and a tendency to temper tantrums.

One result of society regarding slimness as the '**norm**' is that people regarded as overweight are often discriminated against. Court cases have proved that people have not been promoted or been offered a job because they do not conform to a particular ideal appearance. Fashion houses use models of a particular size and advertisements rarely target anyone falling outside this perceived 'perfection'.

As a result other individuals are increasingly disillusioned and militant about the rights they are being denied. People with physical or mental impairments can be excluded from parts of society because it is easier to ignore them than to help them. Young people whose body size or physical looks do not conform with the current fashions can find themselves under enormous pressure.

There are positive aspects to the 'body culture': improving health through diet and fitness are good things. It used to be seen as the job of other people, such as doctors, nurses and employers, to look after the individual's health. Better education now means that people realise they can help themselves and prevent ill-health happening in the first place.

What do you think ?

Fortunately, not everyone is taken in by the 'body beautiful image'. If there is nothing wrong with wanting to look good, where do you draw the line?

Celebrity

Celebrity is like ice cream – It melts!
(David Soul, Actor and Singer)

Celebrity: a well-known person.

People can be very cruel. They don't mean to be. They just don't regard celebrities as real. And I guess, in some ways, we're not.

(Don Johnson, Actor)

This section attempts to trace the development of the 'Celebrity Cult' and to show the difference between celebrity and fame.

What is the difference between a celebrity and someone who is famous? Put simply, famous people are normally those who are known throughout the world, having achieved great success in a chosen area. Celebrities may be well known nationally, but their fame can be short-lived and they are not always important in our lives.

The public's interest in celebrities could be for two reasons: on the one hand, we admire them but, on the other hand, we also resent them because of their apparent lifestyles and wealth. One view of this is that: 'We are always on the outside, our faces pressed against the windows, looking into their world'.

Since the 1980s it has been easy to spot individuals labelled for being 'celebrities', as they appear regularly in the headlines of tabloid newspapers or make frequent television appearances.

IN THE NEWS

One minute here, next minute gone!

The price you pay for being a celebrity

CELEBRITY'S SON COMMITS SUICIDE

1 What do you think David Soul means when he compares celebrity status to ice cream?

Living in the age of celebrity gone mad!

2 What is the main difference between being famous and being a celebrity?

Celebrities guarantee a quick TV ratings fix

3 Look through the headlines. What do they tell us about the problems of being a celebrity?

The entertainment world produces the greatest number of celebrities, some of whom also become very famous. In the past film stars, although popular, were almost untouchable, and were difficult to relate to. As television became popular in the 1950s many more celebrities were created, but unlike the cinema these individuals appeared 'normal', with no mystery about them.

Activities

The individuals in figure **A** are famous and some of them can be regarded as celebrities.

1 After researching the three individuals can you make the distinction?

2 Can you think of other individuals who are famous and have celebrity status?

Due to the power of television and film, celebrities can now be found in all walks of life. The majority come from the worlds of entertainment and sport. Even the sensational style of news coverage producing 'nine day wonder celebrities' can be seen as just another form of entertainment. The media can create a celebrity and they do not even have to be human! In 1996 a cloned sheep called Dolly made all the headlines, just as 30 years earlier a dolphin called Flipper was made a celebrity by starring in a TV series! In the 1970s the racehorse Red Rum would regularly draw crowds as a guest of honour at public events.

A Albert Einstein (top), Elvis Presley (centre) and Mother Teresa (below). Famous, celebrity or both?

The main areas where celebrities are often drawn from   **B**

THINK ABOUT

1 In groups, discuss the six areas highlighted in **B** and try to decide which one produces the most celebrities. Can you think of celebrities who, in your opinion, set bad examples? Who do you think are the most likely individuals to be influenced by celebrities?

Previously people became famous as a result of some outstanding achievement but some individuals today see fame and status as a personal goal. Film stars of 50 years ago wanted to be 'safe and sound' whereas today they are far more likely to be 'famously damaged'. The type of celebrity largely depends on what the public demands. In the 1940s and 1950s most film stars such as John Wayne were 'honest to God' heroes. In contrast, the 1960s saw the creation of the anti-hero or 'rebel', such as James Dean. By the 1980s the public demanded extraordinary heroes performing impossible feats (**C**).

The Three Queens in mourning for King George VI, Queen Elizabeth II, Queen Mary and **D** Queen Mother

The changing faces of **C** heroes: James Dean (above), Arnold Schwarzenegger (right)

The 'celebrity cult' began after the Second World War when people wanted glamour and entertainment. Leading photographers such as Yousuf Karsh provided the pictures in the newspapers and magazines that everyone wanted to see. To have your photo taken by Karsh (to be 'karshed') was proof that an individual was a celebrity. Celebrities were in demand and a new wave of movie-star celebrity magazines were soon appearing in America. In 1954 you could even buy a magazine entitled '3D Star Pin-Ups', which promised celebrity photos 'so real you can almost touch them!' Demand increased for photos of film stars, singers and even members of royalty.

In the early 1950s it was unthinkable that a member of the Royal Family was in any way a celebrity. But an historic photograph taken of the 'Three Queens' (**D**) at the funeral of George VI in 1952 changed the way the public regarded royalty. When published in the newspapers the photo caused hundreds of complaints about the invasion of privacy, and yet today it would be regarded as harmless. By the 1980s members of the Royal Family were no longer regarded as untouchable but were becoming celebrities.

Drugs kill the star beaten by stardom
MARILYN: SUICIDE?

E The cost of celebrity status

Now even politicians and business people can become headline news. The first politician to achieve worldwide celebrity status was probably Sir Winston Churchill, whose photo by Yousuf Karsh was published worldwide as an example of the defiant spirit of Britain during the Second World War. In 1960 Alberto Korda took a photo of the Cuban revolutionary Che Guevara that became the symbol of the 'Revolutionary Sixties'. The image made its subject an instant celebrity.

Both men were more than just celebrities and their many achievements can be read about in history books, but the celebrity status they held was certainly helped by the power of these photographs.

Sometimes someone in the street can find themselves in the public eye. (As Andy Warhol said, 'Everybody will be famous for fifteen minutes'.) Another route to celebrity is through **notoriety**, described as 'the lifeblood of the celebrity'. Certain pop stars in particular deliberately create a reckless image but then have to live up to this 'reputation'. Others, such as the actress Marilyn Monroe, self destruct because they are unable to cope with their fame (**E**). Some individuals, like the billionaire American Howard Hughes, become recluses and refuse to be seen in public. Even then, they earn the title 'celebrity recluse'!

Howard Hughes becomes a recluse

THINK ABOUT

2 Can you think of two individuals who:

a) can be regarded as 'fifteen minute' celebrities?

b) have deliberately taken the notoriety route to gain celebrity status? Give details of your choice.

Activities

3 In pairs or groups brainstorm the responsibilities that you think go with being a 'celebrity'. What happens if people do not take those responsibilities seriously?

4 Role-play a situation where a celebrity and a journalist have been invited to speak on television about the behaviour and the example the celebrity is setting. Before you begin, discuss together the type of questions that the interviewer is going to ask and the possible replies that the two guests will make.

When it comes to creating celebrities, television has replaced photographs. However, it can destroy a celebrity just as easily as it creates one, as many have found out to their cost!

In the 1990s the roles of celebrity and television were almost reversed. Having the right celebrity attached to a project was often the only way to get it taken seriously. In extreme cases the person featuring in the programme becomes more important than the actual subject itself.

In the 1960s the 'celebrity theme' developed further when the film director, Federico Fellini used the phrase 'paparazzi' (italian for little insects) to describe the photographers who pestered the celebrities. The public had always been fascinated by the private lives of famous people but many celebrities no longer wanted sensational headlines, they now valued their privacy. Certain newspapers and magazines however were desperate to obtain exclusive photos of celebrities in order to boost their circulation numbers.

In the 1970s the paparazzi were happy to photograph celebrities coming out of nightclubs or restaurants, but within ten years members of the public were demanding the innermost 'secrets' of the stars. It was claimed that the 1980s saw 'the most exhaustive invasion of privacy in history, with the most intimate details of celebrities' personal lives flashed around the world'.

THINK ABOUT

3 In pairs or groups discuss whether you think people in the public eye should be allowed to have a private life, free from intrusion? Draw up a list of what you see are the advantages and disadvantages of being a celebrity. Choose a spokesperson to report your views to the rest of the class in a report or discussion.

Activities

5 What items in the news recently concern examples of celebrities?

6 Using newspapers and magazines make a collage of headlines of your own choice. You can try to give examples of several individuals or, if you prefer, follow the news items over a period of time on just one person.

By the 1990s there was a huge demand for sensational or explicit photos. As one journalist stated: 'We've done their sexual stuff, we've done their drugs stuff, we've done their adultery, their diseases... what do we do next?' It was clear that the paparazzi 'pests' had become 'a plague' and for the 1990s their main target was the most photographed woman in the world – Diana, Princess of Wales.

There is no better example of the famous person turned 'celebrity' than Princess Diana. Diana's case provides the perfect example of the way today's celebrity is 'slowly stripped bare' before the public gaze. Although she was happy to be in the public eye after her divorce, nothing could have prepared her for the way in which she was pursued by the paparazzi. When she wanted greater privacy she was not allowed to have it. Vast sums of money were on offer to any photographer who could take a compromising picture of her. Eventually, the relentless scramble to obtain these exclusive photos contributed to the events leading to the car crash in which she died in August 1997.

F 2 September 1997

What do you think

Is the price of being a celebrity worth paying? Give reasons for your answer.

Drugs

Drug: a plant or chemical which significantly alters the physical or mental state of its user.

Drugs are about as glamorous as cancer.

(Former drug addict)

The Misuse of Drugs Act has divided society and branded half a generation 'criminal'.

(Simon Jenkins, Journalist)

AIM This unit examines the complexities of drug taking, the factors that lead people to take drugs and the effects of drug abuse.

Drugs of all kinds have been used since earliest recorded history: the cannabis plant for example was used in China over 5,000 years ago, and in 430 BC, the Greek doctor Hippocrates used willow bark to relieve pain for his patients. Islamic cultures added new discoveries to the knowledge of drugs they had gathered from the ancient Chinese and Romans. As science advanced in the 1500s and 1600s, doctors and scientists made important progress in the study of drugs and by the nineteenth century, medicine was revolutionised by the use of drugs. Demand for them has risen throughout the twentieth century.

Outlawing certain drugs is a fairly recent development: opium could be bought in Britain in the late nineteenth century, and obtained as easily as alcohol is today. Artists, writers and politicians used it in an attempt to increase their energy and creativity. Others used it as a way of treating illness because they could not afford a doctor. But by the 1890s the legal availability of opium was restricted because of concern about its habit forming dangers.

In the early twentieth century some 'remedies' contained dangerous drugs and many people developed a dependence on them. Even today, modern medicine relies on legal prescription drugs which can lead to dependency. Some of the most commonly abused non-prescription drugs can be bought legally and include alcohol and tobacco.

In the drugs debate there are three different terms which are often used and need understanding: **addiction**, **dependence** and **abuse**.

Addiction

Being unable to stop taking a drug without suffering unpleasant physical feelings. The person's entire life can centre around buying and taking drugs.

Dependence

A strong urge to keep experiencing the pleasurable effects of a drug or the routine of using it. Dependence can be physical, psychological or both.

Activities

1   Explain in your own words the differences between addiction, dependence and abuse.

2   In Britain alcohol and tobacco kill far more people than all the illegal drugs put together. Why then, do you think they are still legal?

Abuse

There is no one clear definition of this. Often it is a judgement by society about what is the wrong use of drugs. Some people regard abuse as involving any illegal drug, while others may include legal drugs such as alcohol.

There are thousands of different types of drugs in use today. Some are prescribed by doctors for their important medical uses against illness. All medicines are drugs, but not all drugs are medicines. Some drugs are used simply because they make people feel good, or are used out of habit or addiction.

Despite evidence that they can be harmful to health, certain drugs such as alcohol and tobacco are socially acceptable. Statistically alcohol and tobacco represent a greater threat to health than illegal drugs but inevitably, when the debate arises, attention focuses on the abuse of drugs, particularly those which are regarded as illegal.

Unfortunately, in the last 30 years drugs have been presented in a very attractive way, mainly by media marketing. A drug like cocaine has been associated with sex, violence and financial success. Celebrities, often regarded as role models, contribute to this glamorous image and certain illegal drugs have almost been seen as 'fashion accessories'.

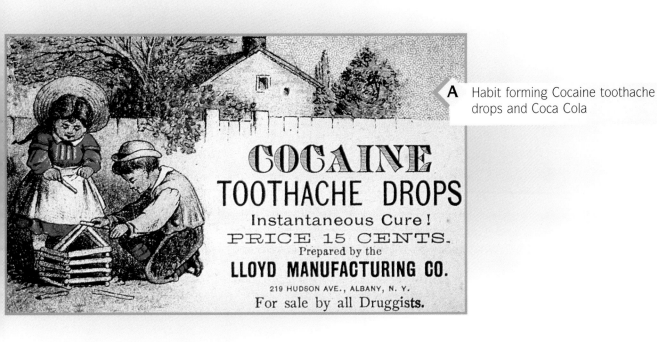

A   Habit forming Cocaine toothache drops and Coca Cola

IN THE NEWS

Legalising drugs – whose side are you on?

SHOCK WARNING ON DRUGS MAY ATTRACT CHILDREN

Unfortunately there is no Trades Description Act for the addict!

ONE IN THREE SMOKE CANNABIS BY THE AGE OF 14

Drug abuse not out of control

1 Why do you think a 'shock warning' might fail to put young people off experimenting with drugs?

2 What issues do you think are being raised by the headline 'Unfortunately there is no Trades Description Act for the addict!'?

In the late 1980s and 1990s a further problem arose in the form of 'designer drugs', so called because they are variations on existing illegal drugs created in laboratories. Often of poor quality they are very dangerous and laws have to be constantly reviewed in order to keep up with them.

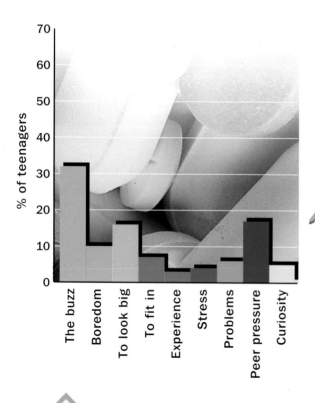

B The reasons young people use drugs

In the 1990s there has been a campaign to legalise certain drugs, especially cannabis. Amongst young people, cannabis is the most widely-used drug, followed by 'hallucinants' such as amphetamines, LSD, magic mushrooms, amyl nitrate and ecstasy. Attention is often focused on the trend of increasing drug use among the young and the possible explanations for it.

Activities

3 In groups, look at figure **B** and discuss what you think are the main reasons why teenagers start using drugs. Produce a group statement summarising your views to present to the rest of the class.

4 Discuss the different situations in which a teenager might be offered drugs. Role-play a scene showing an individual in a situation where some friends are pressurising him/her to take drugs. What are the various tactics the person could use in order to refuse?

Most drugs can be placed under three different categories:

Stimulants

Substances which speed up the nervous system and the way the brain reacts and keep people awake (cocaine, crack, amphetamines (speed), and ecstasy).

Depressants

Chemicals which slow down the way the brain works and cause sleep (heroin).

Hallucinogens

These affect the brain so that the individual starts seeing things differently (LSD, cannabis, magic mushrooms). They cause visions or hallucinations.

The use and abuse of drugs: Ben Johnson (above); Tour de France, 1998 (right)

Many chemicals are habit forming so that a user reaches a stage where they cannot do without them. These people are called drug addicts or drug dependents. Withdrawal is the reaction of the body when regular drug use is stopped. Symptoms can vary from headaches and muscle cramps lasting a few days to death, depending on the drug and the extent of use.

Some drugs, such as anabolic steroids, cannot be categorised easily but are still dangerous when abused. Steroids are sometimes prescribed to treat anaemia, bone disease and breast cancer, and to strengthen muscle for bedridden patients, but they are being used by some athletes and body builders to increase muscle and power. Some steroids became Class A drugs in September 1996 because medical experts were concerned about some side-effects, such as aggressive behaviour and liver damage.

In September 1988, the athlete Ben Johnson was stripped of his Olympic gold medal after he failed a random drugs test (**C**). Today, competitors in most sports are aware that they risk fines, suspensions and, in some cases, life-long disqualification if a test shows they are taking steroids, performance enhancing drugs or drugs taken for 'recreational' purposes such as cannabis. Even using medicinal drugs must be reported to the proper sporting authority. If not, the sports person risks failing a random drugs test and being punished.

The different types of drugs and their risks and effects

	How taken?	*Effects*	*Risks*
Amphetamines	'Speed' is a white/grey powder which can be sniffed, injected or used in tablet form.	Keeps you awake and energetic. Can boost user's confidence and is sometimes used to suppress appetite.	Can cause mood swings, and aggressive behaviour. Users risk becoming physically run down due to lack of sleep and food. Also risk of liver damage and mental illness.
Barbiturates	Usually in tablet form but also available as capsules or syrup. Can be injected.	Helps people to relax. Often prescribed as sleeping tablets.	Users can become very dependent on them. Large doses produce a drunken effect – slurred speech or clumsy actions.
Cannabis	Normally smoked but it can also be brewed into a drink or eaten.	People often become cheerful, talkative and have a greater awareness of sound and colour.	Effects vary according to people's moods. It can disturb concentration, short-term memory loss and slow reaction time. Cannabis has a high tar factor so smoking it can cause lung cancer.
Cocaine	A white powder normally sniffed but can be injected or smoked.	In the short term the drug can create a feeling of well being, indifference to pain and increase self-confidence.	The drug is habit forming and in the long term can be expensive. It can cause paranoia, restlessness, nausea, insomnia and weight loss. It can rot the teeth and the nose lining and has very unpleasant withdrawal symptoms.
Crack	Crack is cocaine that has been processed into crystals for smoking.	Similar effects to cocaine but usually more powerful.	Regular users reduce their ability to communicate effectively and often appear nervous and excitable. Smoking crack can cause various breathing problems and withdrawal can be very unpleasant.
Ecstasy	Ecstasy comes in tablet form, and occasionally in coloured capsules.	The user will often experience a sense of well being and a heightened awareness to those around them.	The drug is a stimulant closely resembling amphetamines or speed. Because it is associated with clubs and raves the most serious danger comes from heat stroke and dehydration – losing too much body fluid by sweating to death and internal bleeding.
GHB	A mixture of solvents and caustic soda. A colourless liquid with a slightly salty taste sold in small bottles or capsules.	It can relax the user and produces feelings similar to alcohol. GHB has gained a reputation as a 'sex drug'.	It has some nasty side-effects such as sickness, shaking of the leg and arm muscles. It can also produce fits and users have been known to collapse and die.

	How taken?	*Effects*	*Risks*
Heroin	In its pure form heroin is a white powder made from the opium poppy. It can be sniffed, injected or smoked.	Produces a feeling of warmth and sleepy contentment.	Heroin is addictive and the user will need to take more and more to get the same 'buzz'. Injecting damages the veins, causing poor circulation, blood clots, abscesses and even gangrene.
LSD	LSD usually comes on small squares of blotting paper called 'tabs' or trips. It can also come in the form of pills or capsules.	A 'trip' can last for up to 36 hours making users hallucinate (see things that are not there or have distorted vision) and lose all sense of time.	The function of the brain can be permanently affected and long-term mental illnesses that are hidden can be triggered. Users do not usually get dependent but flashbacks (reliving the trip) can happen years later without any warning.
Magic Mushrooms	Certain types of mushrooms growing in the wild contain an hallucinogenic drug. They can be eaten raw, cooked, brewed into a tea or preserved by drying.	Sound and vision can be affected and the user can often feel confused and disorientated.	Sometimes sickness, anxiety and panic attacks can occur. Unpleasant hallucinations can be experienced particularly after repeated or unusually high doses. The greatest danger, however, is picking the wrong mushrooms as some species are poisonous.
Poppers	Poppers is the term given for a group of chemicals known as amyl nitrates. Their most common form is as a gold coloured liquid which is inhaled.	Poppers cause immediate effects which last only for a short period of time. Blood pressure is reduced. They are often used to heighten sexual arousal.	Some people experience headaches and sickness and regular use can lead to skin irritation around the nose and mouth. Swallowing poppers can lead to unconsciousness and on rare occasions, death.
Solvents	Solvents are sniffed and can include glues, butane gas, cleaning and correction fluids, paints and petrol.	The effects come on quickly. The experience is like being drunk and users often feel light headed and dizzy and can experience hallucinations.	They can cause users to feel sick and very drowsy. There is a risk of death through choking on vomit or heart failure. The misuse of solvents is more likely to kill than any other illegal drug including heroin.
Tranquillisers	Commonly prescribed man-made drug used to treat depression, stress, anxiety and insomnia. Usually in tablet or capsule form.	They can cause drowsiness and can relieve anxiety but it is easy to become dependent on them.	Can cause memory lapse and blurred vision. Large doses can be very dangerous especially when mixed with alcohol.

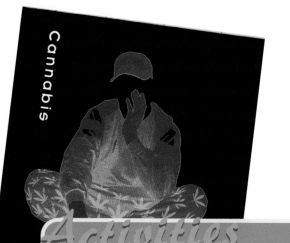

The Medicines Act 1968 and the Misuse of Drugs Act 1971 are the main laws covering drug use. Medicinal drugs available on doctor's prescriptions or bought in chemists are controlled by the Medicines Act. The Misuse of Drugs Act bans the non-medical use of certain drugs. Legally there are three distinct classes of drug: **A** (ecstasy, cocaine, LSD and heroin); **B** (cannabis and barbiturates) and **C** (tranquillisers and mild amphetamines). Any controlled drug prepared for injection counts as Class A. The penalties for drug offences are often severe and vary according to the offence and the class of drug being used. Class A drugs carry the highest penalty.

Activities

5 Why do you think the images on the three cards have been used?

6 Choose a particular drug and create your own design for a card warning about the dangers.

7 What effect do drug laws have? Do they act as a deterrent, and what effect do they have on the way users obtain and take drugs?

8 What are the arguments for and against allowing people to legally use drugs in small amounts for their own personal use?

D Images of drugs

The effects of any drug on an individual depends on three things:

- what the drug is (the amount taken, the strength of it and whether it is used by itself or with other drugs);

- who is using it (different users will have different experiences);

- the situation (the effects may be different if the user is alone or with others, and can depend on where the drug is being used).

When drugs are used certain practices become more dangerous. There are risks relating to the drug itself; these may be physical, psychological or both. Becoming dependent may present financial risks as drug habits are expensive. Some drugs can lead to changes in lifestyle which damage family and friendships. Withdrawal symptoms resulting from stopping long-term use of some drugs can be unpleasant and difficult to cope with. There are other health problems as well as those posed by the drug itself: sharing needles for injection can transmit diseases such as HIV and hepatitis. In response, health authorities in Britain have encouraged addicts not to share needles and to dispose of them carefully. Needle and syringe exchange schemes have helped to prevent the spread of infection.

E How drugs can affect an individual's life

F Why do people take drugs?

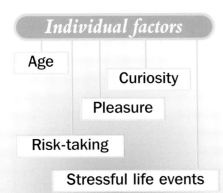

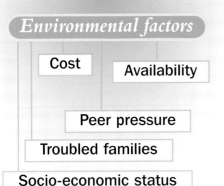

*Under each of the five headings shown in **E**, examine ways in which a person's life can be disrupted through a dependency on drugs.*

Below are ten statements, the answers for which can be found in this unit. On your own write down whether you think they are true or false. Then with the group or a partner check your answers and discuss what you have learned about drugs. Which facts did you find the most surprising, and which the most worrying?

1 *A drug alters the physical or mental state of the user.*
2 *Drugs have been used for thousands of years.*
3 *The practice of medicine was revolutionised by the use of drugs in the sixteenth century.*
4 *Cocaine was once used in Coca Cola and toothache drops.*
5 *Dependence on a drug is always physical.*
6 *The most dangerous drugs can be bought legally.*
7 *Ecstasy is the most commonly used drug amongst young people.*
8 *Heroin is a stimulant.*
9 *LSD is a depressant.*
10 *Drugs are grouped into two legal classes.*

The reasons for drug use usually involve a combination of individual and environmental factors (**F**), but nevertheless many people continue using drugs because they become dependent or addicted to them.

What do you think

A recent article on drug addiction was titled, 'Sometimes other problems have to be solved first'. What do you think this meant?

Environment

> Man marks the Earth with ruin.
>
> (Lord Byron, Poet, 1788–1824)

Environment: the natural world – the land, the seas, the air, and all creatures and plants.

> If we are to protect and preserve our environment on a global scale, we all must do our part, as nations, as families and as individuals.
>
> (Al Gore, Vice President of the USA)

AIM This section looks at the evidence which suggests that we have caused great harm to the Earth's environment and examines ways in which some of the damage is now being repaired.

We are informed that life first appeared on earth about 3,000 million years ago. Since then it has evolved into literally millions of different forms. All these species live in natural balance with one another but one species threatens to unsettle this balance: humans.

Our actions today are making the planet Earth less and less pleasant to live on. The natural resources that took millions of years to develop have been damaged and depleted because of our failure to use them effectively. Ultimately, the earth simply will not be able to support life.

PROLOGUE

Child of the Future?

The young boy awoke on a hot, oppressive morning. It wasn't a school day, so he could afford to lie back for a while with his favourite storybook. That was the one with drawings of the great forests – the woodlands filled with tall trees, wild animals and clear-running streams. The scenes seemed so magical that the boy could hardly believe in them, though his parents assured him that such wonders once existed.

Closing his book, he saw no joy in the day ahead. He wished the air conditioner wasn't broken. He wished there was more food in the refrigerator. He wished he could see the great forests. But there was no use in thinking about that now. It was enough of a struggle just to be alive.

THINK ABOUT

1   In small groups read through the story 'The Prologue'. Discuss how we can encourage more people to see the importance of protecting the environment. In what practical ways can we help to preserve the Earth?

IN THE NEWS

The world is dying – who cares?

ATOLL NATIONS GET THAT SINKING FEELING

CONSERVATION OR CATASTROPHE!

Wildlife feels the heat from our climate folly

Scientists warn of threat to Arctic ozone

1 All five headlines give clear warning signs. Select any one of them and design a logo which could be used by an environmental group.

2 Look around the room you are sitting in. How many items are made from wood? How many pieces of equipment use up valuable energy?

Many groups have expressed concerns about global climate change and the exploitation of limited resources. Scientists have repeatedly warned of the climatic changes that will be seen in the twenty-first century. As figure **A** shows, the global temperatures are steadily rising.

Experts are alarmed by the evidence of global warming and its effects. A gradual rise in sea levels already threatens hundreds of populated atoll islands (**B**) and it is estimated that by the year 2050 huge sums of money will have to be spent on new coastal defences as the sea levels continue to rise. The tropical forests that help to soak up the carbon dioxide mankind places in the atmosphere are being destroyed. It is predicted that starvation, particularly in Africa, will increase and over 100 million more people will be facing drought conditions.

In 1992 leaders from 178 nations met in Rio de Janeiro for the Earth Summit, to make agreements that would help protect and preserve the global environment. Unfortunately, in many cases we have seen that words have not been backed up by action.

In 1997 leading environmental experts, scientists and politicians gathered for a ten day summit in the Japanese city of Kyoto. Their aim was to prevent the main threats to the world environment: **global warming**, **ozone depletion**, deforestation and desertification All four threats are interconnected and all must be addressed to avoid further damage to our environment.

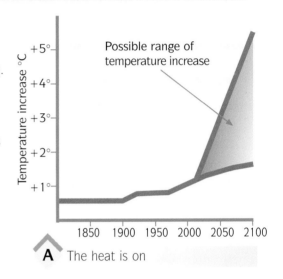

Possible range of temperature increase

A The heat is on

THINK ABOUT

2 In small groups discuss why it is so difficult to get governments to agree environmental policies when nearly everyone agrees that the environment needs protecting.

3 Choose one of the four threats examined at the Kyoto summit and design and produce a wallchart to explain the damage that is being done to the environment.

B Will rising sea levels submerge this island?

The problems facing the environment basically break down into 11 distinct categories. The following table illustrates the worrying changes in these areas between the 1970s and the 1990s. However there are now signs of improvement in all categories, which provides hope for the twenty-first century.

How the world has changed

	1972	1997	Facts
Population	3.84 billion, of whom 72% lived in the developing countries.	Global population is 5.85 billion, 80% living in developing countries.	Global population increases by 80 million a year, so more agricultural land is needed for new homes. Birth rates however are unexpectedly dropping due to increased birth control. The average number of children per woman has dropped to 2.9 from 4.2 in 1985.
War and refugees	Nations spent $836 billion on arms, refugees numbered 3 million.	Military spending now $800 billion. 26 million refugees.	Wars destroy land and leave it unusable for years afterwards. Dense jungle and forests are easily destroyed. As the twenty-first century approaches, however, fewer destructive wars are being fought. There are greater efforts to avoid the brutality of war.
Transport	250 million motor vehicles – pollution mainly confined in the developed countries.	500 million vehicles – third world cities increasingly polluted by road traffic.	In Bangkok, each driver spends the equivalent of 44 days per year in traffic jams, resulting in poor air quality and millions of lost working hours. Some great megacities, like Los Angeles, are overcoming such problems with greater fuel efficiency, the fitting of catalytic converters on car engines, and better use of public transport.
Nuclear reactors	Just over 100 reactors generated electricity in 15 countries.	443 reactors in 31 countries generating 17% of the world's electricity.	Nuclear power plants put out almost no carbon dioxide and so the greenhouse effect is limited. On the other hand, threats of accidents such as Chernobyl and the dangers of nuclear waste have led to reviews on the construction of new nuclear power plants. Alternative power sources such as solar and wind generated electricity are now being more seriously examined.
Global warming	16 billion tonnes of carbon dioxide released into the air.	Rise in annual release of carbon dioxide now over 23 billion tonnes.	The presence of greenhouse gases is essential to life, otherwise the earth would be 33°C cooler. The problem is that greenhouse-gas concentrations have become too high, resulting in long-term climate change. Leaders of the developed nations are committed to ensuring that by the year 2012 emissions of greenhouse gases are reduced to the 1990 level.
Ozone layer and chlorine	Chlorine concentration was 1.4 parts per billion. Holes in the ozone layer were as yet unknown.	Chlorine level doubled to over 3 parts per billion. Ozone holes will continue for decades to come.	The 'ozone' layer filters dangerous ultra violet rays from the sun. Holes have been caused by chemicals such as chlorofluorocarbons (CFCs) found in aerosol sprays and refrigerators. As CFCs are phased out scientists hope that the ozone layer will start recovering and regain its 1979 level by the year 2030.

	1972	*1997*	*Facts*
Megacities	Three cities with over 10 million inhabitants – two in the developing countries.	18 cities with over 10 million people – 13 of them in developing countries.	Cities like Tokyo, Bombay and Dhaka cannot cope with millions of tons of household refuse. Breathing the air in New Delhi is equal to smoking 10–20 cigarettes a day! Projects such as avoiding traffic congestion, clean-up campaigns, improved sanitation and vaccination programmes have helped many of the megacities to cope with environmental threats.
Rainforests	About 0.5% of the world's rainforests were being lost each year – over 100,00 sq kms, an area the size of Iceland.	Further increase to 130,000 sq kms per year – as a result it is thought that one or two plants become extinct every hour.	In the last 100 years about 40% of the tropical rainforests have been destroyed. Trees are felled to provide fuel, land for farming, and products such as paper and construction timber. Although many countries still refuse to co-operate, international pressure is beginning to lead to forest-regeneration schemes.
Fisheries	Around 58 million tonnes of fish were taken from the oceans.	Estimates taken in 1997 suggest that over 90 million tonnes were taken.	Overfishing is a serious problem as millions of tonnes of non-target fish are caught and accidently killed. As oceans are used as giant dustbins, marine life is threatened. The United Nations declared 1998 the Year of the Oceans and established over 1,200 protected coastal zones.
Species	Thousands of species endangered. Estimated that about two million elephants were left.	Elephant numbers estimated between 286,000 and 580,000. Globally hundreds of species face extinction.	Certain species of animals are at the point of extinction because of hunting, urbanisation and agriculture. In just over 100 years the North American bison was reduced from 60 million to less than 600. Environmental groups such as Greenpeace, Friends of the Earth, WWF and RSPCB are working to ensure the survival of endangered species.
Water	Each year a total of 2,600 cubic kilometres of fresh water was being used, mostly for irrigation.	Consumption now is nearly 4,200 cubic kilometres a year. Over 1.4 billion people have no access to safe drinking water.	All kinds of waste including human sewage, toxic chemicals and nuclear waste contaminate our land, rivers and seas. One estimate is that half the people in the developing world are suffering from a water-related sickness. Industrial water recycling, drip irrigation and careful conservation is now encouraged by an increasing number of nations.

C Clear signs of danger: a computer enhanced picture of the ozone hole over the Earth.

D The number of megacities like Tokyo is increasing, and placing more strain on the environment around them

E Environmental pressure also threatens species, such as the polar bear, turtle, ocelot and rhino

Activities

1 According to experts if the world population continues to rise at its present rate it will have doubled by the year 2525. In groups, or on your own, brainstorm for five minutes on what you think life will be like then.

2 Organise a survey in your year group to see if people are using CFC-friendly products.

3 Look at the cartoon (**F**). What message is the artist trying to make?

4 'Rainforests are being cleared to make room for cattle ranching and to produce timber.' In twos, role-play a situation where one of you is explaining to a peasant farmer why he should not cut down the forest on the edge of his farm. What arguments do you think the farmer might make?

F Is this what the earth will soon look like?

EPILOGUE

Child of the Future?

The young girl awoke on a cool, inviting morning. It wasn't a school day, so she could look forward to doing what she liked best. Her family was going just outside the city into the great forest, where they would stroll under the tall trees, spot wild animals and wade in the clear-running streams.

Every time they went, she felt lucky. After all, her parents had told her stories about the old days – before people learned to protect the land and water and harness the power of wind and sunlight. It was a dark time when the forests died, rivers ran dry and millions went hungry. The girl was amazed and frightened that such things could ever have happened. But there was no need to think about that now not with a glorious day ahead. It was so good to be alive.

What do you think?

Read the extract 'The Epilogue'. What do we need to do to ensure that the story comes true?

Family

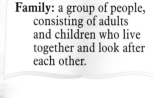

Family: a group of people, consisting of adults and children who live together and look after each other.

All happy families resemble one another, but each unhappy family is unhappy in its own way.

(Leo Tolstoy, Author)

If men and women are to live the same lives, the family must be abolished.

(Plato, Philosopher)

AIM The main aim is to illustrate that a 'family' has different forms but it exists in most societies and seems to suit the needs of most people.

How to define what is meant by 'family' is not easy as it can mean many things, but usually it refers to those immediate relatives with whom you live. It can also include all those people to whom you are related either by birth or marriage.

Family life

The family is the first social group to which most people belong and is very important in the development of every individual's life. Family members form close emotional ties which, in a good or bad way, are likely to affect the relationships they have through life. The family is often the base from where you learn everything in life.

C The role of the family

B Learning to share

It teaches us about the traditions and customs of society.

It teaches us how we are expected to behave (a process called socialisation) and prepares us for the later roles in our lives.

It provides legal and economic rights and responsibilities.

The role of the FAMILY

It provides security.

We learn about relationships and how to deal with others.

It forms the group in which most humans spend a lot of time.

It allows wealth and property to be passed on through generations.

It provides security for having and bringing up children.

The family gives us a sense of belonging and identity.

It provides a good way of caring for the young and old.

HAHAHAHA

THINK ABOUT

1 Look at figure **C**. What do you think are the three most important roles of the family? Explain your choices.

2 Why do many people think the family is important? What do you think?

Activities

1 'A family is a married couple with their children who live together.'
   a) Write down the types of family that are not included in this definition.
   b) Write or describe your own definition that includes all family types.

2 Choose any two of the family types and show what you think are the advantages and disadvantages of belonging to them.

3 Advertisements on television can give a stereotyped image of family life. In pairs describe a number of advertisements appearing on television which depict a family. Make a chart setting out the information as follows:

Advert	Type of family	Children	Product

Do any of the adverts reflect real family life?

IN THE NEWS

MEN WHO COPE ALONE

Changing roles in the family

The problem of the latch key children

SINGLE MOTHERS LEFT TO STRUGGLE

Stay-at-home mothers feel 'second class'

1 It is said that one happy parent is better than two unhappy ones. Do you agree?

2 Do you think a child always needs two parents? Give reasons for your answer.

Traditionally the terms **nuclear** and **extended** have been used to describe family structures. Today four other terms have come into use: reconstituted (step), one-parent, expanded and common law.

Nuclear

This family is a nucleus – a small centre quite separate from other families. It is still the most common form depicted in the media: husband, wife and children living together.

Extended

This family has several generations possibly living in the same household, with other relatives living nearby. This is very common in some societies, but not so much in Britain.

Reconstituted (step)

When a marriage ends, children are often brought up in a situation where at least one parent has re-married.

One-parent

The increasing number of divorces means many children are brought up by one parent alone, usually the mother.

Expanded

Some people choose to live together within a community and share responsibilities and child care. A well-known example of this is the Israeli **kibbutz**.

Common law

Couples live together (cohabit) in stable relationships without feeling the need to get married.

What society chooses to call 'the family' has been under question recently, and it is a subject of concern for many people raising many important questions. Is the family less important now, and does it still offer secure and important values to its members? Are parents increasingly irresponsible? Is marriage on its way out? Is the family really to blame for youth crime, domestic violence and the many other problems of modern society? Before answering these questions it is important to realise that attitudes to marriage, sex and relationships have all changed a great deal throughout the twentieth century.

In Britain families are becoming smaller and the roles within them have changed: many women work and men are no longer seen as the main wage earners. Household jobs are shared more than they used to be and children have more say in what they do and also enjoy far greater freedom. Many women who are wage earners plan their families. There are 'teenage mothers' but, increasingly, many women have their first child much later in life having established a career. With these changing roles there are new problems for families to overcome. Some of these are set out in figure **D** on the right.

Lack of parental support

Addictions

Violence

Divorce

Generation gap

Unwanted children

Poverty

Illness

Poor housing

Unemployment

D Family problems

Activities

4 Look at figure **D**. Can you think of any other family problems? Which issues do you think cause the most arguments in a family?

5 In groups of four, take roles as a grandparent, a mother, a father and a teenager. Act out a situation where the teenager wants to go to a party and then stay overnight at a friend's house. Explore the different attitudes. Do the parents support one another? Who does the grandparent support?

6 Imagine a situation where a single parent has a demanding teenager, who constantly wants more money for clothes, or to stay out late every night. What are the problems for both sides? How can they be avoided?

What do you think ?

What has brought about changes in the structure of the family in Britain?

Almost everyone belongs to some kind of 'family', but most families are not the perfect ones depicted in adverts. Unfortunately the mistakes of one generation are often repeated by the next generation. As well as being creative and positive, family life can also be very destructive.

Genetics

> *Make no mistake: gene technology has the power to cure, feed, alter and destroy us.*
>
> (Dr Patrick Dixon, Genetics Expert and Author)

Genetics: the study of heredity – how the characteristics of living organisms are passed on from one generation to another.

> *Developments in genetic engineering may soon transform the treatment of human disease at every stage of life, from conception of an embryo through to old age.*
>
> (Peter Moore, Author)

AIM In this section we will be examining how the science of genetics relates to the well-being of people, animals and nature.

New scientific techniques are helping to achieve the ultimate aims of medicine – preserving life and acting in the interests of sufferers of incurable illness and hereditary disease. Despite these worthy aims, recent medical advances often generate strong feelings and arouse widespread publicity and excitement.

The main concern is that we can hardly keep pace with these advances, and that guidelines balancing what we can do with what we should do need constant updating. There are regular calls for tighter regulations and laws in order to keep control on the progress being made.

Many scientists are excited about these new developments and see the possibility of great benefits from the combination of biology and technology. The worries expressed about these advances are often put down to ignorance and misinformation mainly due to sensational headlines in the media.

IN THE NEWS

Yesterday's science fiction is today's reality

MORE TO LIFE THAN A BAG OF GENES!

Hope for endangered species

FRANKENSTEIN'S VEGETABLES!

Medical advances put under the microscope

1 What dangers are being expressed in these headlines?

2 What do you think is meant by the word 'Frankenstein' in one of the headlines?

The British medical profession agrees on a general principle which is based on maintaining 'the utmost respect for human life from the time of commencement [of treatment]'. With new medical technology, however, it is not always easy for doctors to decide how to act for the best. Medical advances made over the past three decades have re-focused the whole debate: medication, life support machines and transplants can keep people alive who would have previously died. Today, at the centre of the debate, lies genetic engineering which many believe will revolutionise biological and medical science and will undoubtedly alter our lives in the twenty-first century.

In the 1950s two scientists, James Watson and Francis Crick, unravelled the double-helix or 'spiral staircase' structure of DNA (deoxyribonucleic acid). This is the chemical used by animals and plants to store the information that is passed from generation to generation. The structure of DNA and its organisation into genes and chromosomes has led to the current revolution in modern genetics.

Every cell in an organism, whether it is a plant, animal or human, contains a complete set of genes known as the genome. The human body is made up of approximately 100 million million cells. The genome of each human cell is made up of 23 pairs of chromosomes.

Each chromosome consists of two long DNA molecules, folded together in a double helix or spiral shape containing up to 4,000 genes. Each gene is a tiny segment of DNA and contains the instructions for the development of a particular inherited characteristic (for example, eye colour). The inheritance of all our characteristics is dependent on genes and chromosomes.

In the 1980s scientists found ways of studying DNA so that they could begin to identify individual human genes. They are now attempting to find the locations of all the genes (there are about 100,000) a process known as 'mapping' and gradually unravelling the structure of each gene, a task known as 'sequencing'. They are discovering which genes are responsible for particular characteristics such as height, eye colour and intelligence as well as finding out more about the 'rogue' genes responsible for so many inherited disorders. The Human Genome Project is the name given to this worldwide research programme.

The task of finding a gene responsible for a particular human disease has been described by one scientist as 'searching for a burnt-out light bulb in a house with no address in an unknown street in an anonymous city in a foreign country'. Despite this, scientists have already linked over 4,000 diseases with genetic faults.

The human genome   **A**

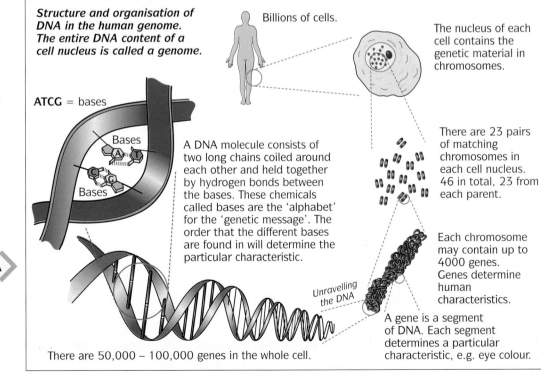

Structure and organisation of DNA in the human genome. The entire DNA content of a cell nucleus is called a genome.

Billions of cells.

The nucleus of each cell contains the genetic material in chromosomes.

ATCG = bases

Bases

Bases

A DNA molecule consists of two long chains coiled around each other and held together by hydrogen bonds between the bases. These chemicals called bases are the 'alphabet' for the 'genetic message'. The order that the different bases are found in will determine the particular characteristic.

There are 23 pairs of matching chromosomes in each cell nucleus. 46 in total, 23 from each parent.

Each chromosome may contain up to 4000 genes. Genes determine human characteristics.

Unravelling the DNA

A gene is a segment of DNA. Each segment determines a particular characteristic, e.g. eye colour.

There are 50,000 – 100,000 genes in the whole cell.

The Human Genome Organisation (HUGO) supervises the findings of scientists working worldwide and ensures work is not duplicated in different countries. The eventual map and sequence of the genome will hopefully allow doctors one day to obtain a genetic read-out of their patients, giving details about inherited features that could lead to ill health in later life.

A 'handbook of human life' would be invaluable for understanding the workings of the human body and for diagnosing and treating human genetic disorders. Inherited diseases could one day be treated by altering the genes that determine our physical make-up (gene therapy).

The nature of the human genome – DNA, genes and chromosomes:

- Each cell contains genetic material in chromosomes.
- A human has 23 pairs of matching chromosomes in each cell nucleus, one of each pair being inherited from each parent.
- Each chromosome consists of DNA.
- Each chromosome contains up to 4,000 genes which determine the physical characteristics of an individual.
- Faults in genes can cause inherited disorders.
- The complete set of this genetic information is contained in 70,000–100,000 genes which make up the human genome.

THINK ABOUT

It is possible that science may one day enable parents to influence the behaviour and appearance of a child by changing or altering certain genes. In a Gallup Poll, individuals were asked about the idea of changing a child's genes:

Characteristics to be altered	Respondents in Poll %	Men %	Women %
Reduce risk of cancer	80	83	77
Reduce the risk of heart disease	76	78	74
Improve eyesight	66	72	60
Reduce the chance of alcoholism	57	61	54
Reduce aggression	54	57	52
Increase intelligence	45	53	37
Reduce the chance of homosexuality	36	43	29
Improve physical strength	27	33	21
Increase physical attractiveness	19	26	13

1 Looking through the nine suggestions, which do you think are the most and least important?

2 Do you notice any significant difference between the answers given by the men and women?

3 Do any of the figures set out above surprise you? If so, which one(s)?

It is important to remember that the ethical issues relating to the uses of genetic engineering can be applied to three main groups: a) humans; b) animals and c) plants (**B**).

The major uses of genetic engineering   **B**

GENETIC ENGINEERING

Treating human and animal diseases

Increasing food production from plants and animals

Reducing the need for harmful chemicals such as pesticides

Development in forensic science

Manufacturing fuels to replace oil

Providing insight into the growth process of cells

Improving processing techniques for food and drugs

THINK ABOUT

4 Examine figure **B** and decide which of these uses are the most important and which get the most negative publicity. In pairs or groups discuss and give reasons for your choices.

C   The benefits of genetic engineering in the plant and animal world?

Genetic engineering can develop 'transgenic' plants that grow faster or produce greater numbers of bigger fruit or even resist disease. The same techniques can also increase animal breeding programmes: animals are being engineered to produce more milk, meat, wool or eggs. Potentially these genetically engineered plants and animals could help solve food shortages in parts of the world.

In 1995 an American company called Calgene produced a new tomato – the Flavr Savr – which was engineered to have a better flavour at the end of its extended shelf life. In 1996 the American chemical giant Monsanto, developed a low-water, 'quick fry' potato with an improved texture. Genetic engineering can now allow scientists to develop new types of plant with built in defences against pests and diseases which still destroy one third of all crops grown. At the same time, however, there is a need for caution because this is not a precise science. Mistakes will be made and no one knows what sort of side-effects genetic engineering may cause in the long term.

Some scientists think that we are experimenting with nature. Already, there are 'super pests' emerging that still attack the supposedly pest-resistant crops. The genes which give transgenic crops their resistance could cross-pollinate with weeds, making them harder to keep under control. New plant viruses could wipe out whole crops with terrible consequences for those whose lives depend on the harvests. Thanks to genetic engineering crops like sugar cane or cocoa will be able to be grown anywhere, but equally this might destroy millions of livelihoods dependent on these crops.

An additional problem is that there is a question of ownership of **patents** and huge financial rewards. Most biotech research has been put into just a few of the most profitable crops such as cotton, tobacco, maize, potato and soya bean. Monsanto holds a patent on all genetically engineered cotton in the United States and Europe: any further research in this area can be done only with their permission and financial agreement.

During the 1990s, genetic research that could not go ahead on humans has often been carried out on animals. Animals have been created with defective human genes, such as cystic fibrosis and cancer, so medical researchers can experiment with them and get a better understanding of the diseases. The rise in demand for human transplant organs has led to animals being engineered and bred to provide suitable organs for transplant (xenotransplants). These could save many lives but there remain real dangers of disease transmission from the animals to humans.

One such warning came when researchers inserted genes for the human growth hormone into pigs, trying to produce bigger animals with leaner meat. The result was the 'Beltsville Pig' which suffered from such severe arthritis that it could not stand. Other experimental breeding policies have proved equally disastrous. The double-muscled 'Belgian Blue' cattle (**C**) can scarcely walk and its calves are so big they have to be delivered by caesarean.

Less controversial are the experiments where there is little or no suffering to the animals and the potential human benefits are massive. Transgenic sheep can produce human proteins in their milk: they are just like normal sheep except that they produce a vital drug, AAT, which is used in treating patients with emphysema, a lung disease.

THINK ABOUT

5 In small groups discuss what the main benefits are of creating 'model' laboratory animals. Should we allow animals to be designed for **a)** medical research and **b)** agricultural benefit?

6 Look back at the quote by Dr Patrick Dixon at the start of this unit. Can you now explain how gene technology has the power to cure, feed, alter and destroy us? List your answers in a table like the one below:

Cure	Feed	Alter	Destroy

Activities

1 Some people argue that any suffering caused to animals is more than outweighed by the benefits of reducing human suffering. Do you agree? Give reasons for your answer.

2 Role-play a discussion between a genetic scientist and a reporter who is opposed to the scientist's work. The scientist is arguing that the benefits of genetic engineering outweigh the dangers and side-effects, but the reporter is not convinced.

We now have the ability and knowledge to alter the very basis of life itself. Designer animals, plants and humans can now be created, together with hundreds of new medical cures. As they unravel the secrets of life however scientists must be cautious, ensuring that they use new knowledge sensibly.

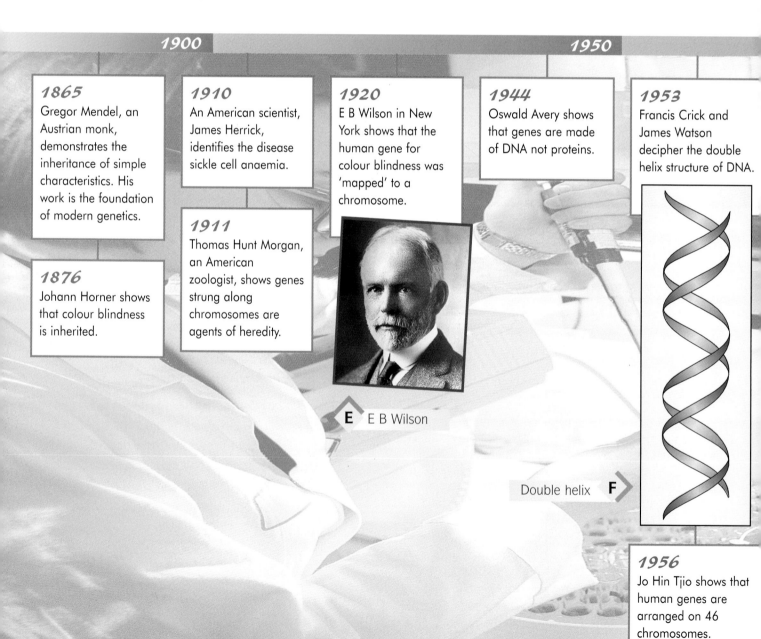

1900

1950

1865
Gregor Mendel, an Austrian monk, demonstrates the inheritance of simple characteristics. His work is the foundation of modern genetics.

1876
Johann Horner shows that colour blindness is inherited.

1910
An American scientist, James Herrick, identifies the disease sickle cell anaemia.

1911
Thomas Hunt Morgan, an American zoologist, shows genes strung along chromosomes are agents of heredity.

1920
E B Wilson in New York shows that the human gene for colour blindness was 'mapped' to a chromosome.

1944
Oswald Avery shows that genes are made of DNA not proteins.

1953
Francis Crick and James Watson decipher the double helix structure of DNA.

E   E B Wilson

Double helix   F

1956
Jo Hin Tjio shows that human genes are arranged on 46 chromosomes.

What do you think ?

Is the likely benefit from genetic engineering greater than the risk?

 D Milestones in genetic engineering

2000

1973
Scientists assemble a genetic 'tool kit' for cutting up DNA in the test tube. The 'birth' of genetic engineering.

1982
The first 'test tube' plants appear.

1984
Robert Sinsheimer proposes an institute to research the human genetic 'blueprint'.

1986
Scientists identify the gene for muscular dystrophy.

1988
James Watson is appointed to head the Human Genome Project with the aim of analysing the structure and arrangement of all human genes.

1989
Discovery of the gene responsible for cystic fibrosis and the p53 gene which suppresses cancer growth.

1990
The first transgenic crops are grown in China.

1991
Researchers in London find the gene which determines maleness and switch the sex of a mouse embryo from female to male.

1992
The first 'map' of the human genome is produced in France.

1993
Gene for Huntingdon's disease is found.

1996
Dolly, a cloned sheep, is born at the Roslin Institute in Scotland.

G Laboratory mouse

H_{IV}

The enemy is not so much HIV itself as it is the unshakeable conviction of the media, public opinion, my father, all my friends and allies – when they're being honest with themselves – a conviction that part of me shares: that AIDS, as the press keeps repeating, 'Is an illness that is always rapidly fatal and for which there is no cure'.

(Emmanuel Dreuilhe, Author)

HIV: the abbreviation for Human Immunodeficiency Virus.

The real tragedy of AIDS lies in the racism, homophobia and negative responses of government, the mainstream medical establishment and society at large.

(Kris Peterson and Corey Dubin)

AIM The unit examines how people's behaviour and attitudes have changed over the last twenty years in response to the crisis caused by the AIDS epidemic.

The first rumours of a 'gay plague' began in New York and San Francisco in 1981 and quickly attracted media attention. Initially reported as a rare type of pneumonia found in five gay men in Los Angeles, the illness was called GRID (Gay Related Immuno Deficiency). But as more cases appeared among heterosexuals, **intravenous** drug users, and children born to infected mothers it was clear that anyone was at risk. Then in December 1982, the first documented case of AIDS (Acquired Immune Deficiency Syndrome) resulting from a blood transfusion led to a US Government warning about contaminated blood supplies.

Although there has been much debate about the origins of HIV, unfortunately there has been a lot of misinformation. In 1998 American scientists reported that the origin of the

A Life cycle of the AIDS virus

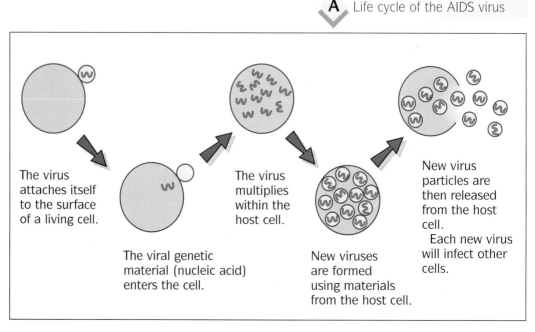

The virus attaches itself to the surface of a living cell.

The viral genetic material (nucleic acid) enters the cell.

The virus multiplies within the host cell.

New viruses are formed using materials from the host cell.

New virus particles are then released from the host cell.
   Each new virus will infect other cells.

AIDS epidemic had been found in a genetic analysis of HIV positive blood taken from an African man in 1959. They suggested that the single virus which began the epidemic probably existed around or just after the Second World War. However it is the 1980s which is recognized as THE decade of HIV and AIDS. Even today we live in the shadow of this epidemic.

AIDS is caused by a virus called HIV (Human Immunodeficiency Virus). In 1983 researchers in France and the United States discovered this virus, which infects a type of white blood cell known as helper T-cells. A person can be infected for many years while remaining healthy and not realise that there is anything wrong. As the virus gradually multiplies in the body it eventually destroys the body's natural defence mechanisms. White blood cells are essential to the body's immune system and as the virus destroys these cells, the body is less able to fight infection. Consequently, people who develop AIDS are far more at risk from infections which normally they would easily resist.

Over the last twenty years millions of people worldwide have contracted HIV. The virus can be transmitted from one person to another in four main ways:

● through unprotected sexual intercourse;

● by drug users sharing equipment such as syringes and needles;

● by operations using infected blood or organ transplants;

● from an infected mother to her baby during pregnancy, or by breast feeding.

In most developed countries blood and body organs are now carefully screened. So apart from sharing infected needles, the main way that an individual is at risk is through unprotected sex and children born to mothers with the virus. HIV can be transferred through bodily fluids that are exchanged such as blood, semen, and breast milk. Any practice that draws blood carries a risk: for example, body-piercers and tattooists must ensure that their equipment is sterilised to very high hygiene standards.

Fortunately HIV is fragile and cannot survive outside body fluids for long. It cannot be transmitted by the following:

NO TRANSMISSION

Touching

Kissing

Bodily contact

Toilet seats

Swimming pools

Coughing and sneezing

Cutlery and food

Pets

Mosquitoes and other insects

Sharing baths/showers

Drinking from the same glass or cup

 B No transmission

Sexual promiscuity, which was not uncommon in certain 'gay communities' in the early 1980s, probably contributed to the early spread of HIV. Unfortunately, the belief that only homosexuals were being infected led to homophobia (fear of homosexuals). Later, this became a fear of anyone suffering from HIV/AIDS. As we discovered more about the virus people realised that it was essential that both homosexuals and heterosexuals practised 'safe sex'.

Activities

1 Can you think of some of the misinformation that surrounds the HIV/AIDS issue?

2 What do the abbreviations HIV and AIDS stand for?

3 Who is most at risk of contracting HIV?

4 What is HIV and how is it transmitted?

5 Explain why HIV spread so rapidly throughout the world.

6 Design a poster aimed at teenagers: 'How to reduce the risk of HIV infection'.

IN THE NEWS

AIDS nurse hits out at 'sick hate letters'

COCKTAIL THAT CHEATS DEATH

AIDS is everybody's business

AIDS Poll reveals ignorance

WORLD AIDS DAY IS MARKED AROUND THE WORLD

1 In small groups read these headlines. In your opinion, which headlines express hope for the future? What do you think is meant by the headline: 'AIDS is everybody's business'? Do you think that knowing more about HIV and AIDS would cause people to change their behaviour?

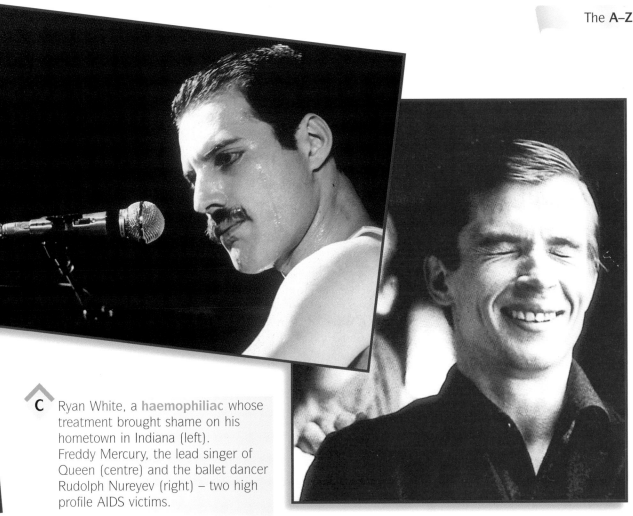

C   Ryan White, a **haemophiliac** whose
treatment brought shame on his
hometown in Indiana (left).
Freddy Mercury, the lead singer of
Queen (centre) and the ballet dancer
Rudolph Nureyev (right) – two high
profile AIDS victims.

Despite the efforts of scientists, the medical profession and health education campaigns,
some people still live in ignorance of HIV and AIDS. Discrimination against sufferers has
been widespread from individuals as well as major institutions. Just the mere fact that an
individual has had an HIV test, no matter what the result, can often disqualify someone
from applying for a mortgage or life insurance policy. One of the hardest things about living
with HIV or AIDS is coping with other people's fear, blame and rejection.

As the epidemic increased in the early 1980s there were examples of terrible behaviour
towards AIDS victims regardless of how they had contracted the virus. One of the worst was
the case of Ryan White who died in April 1990. He was a haemophiliac who contracted
AIDS from a blood transfusion when a child. Parents refused to allow their children to
associate with him and he was forced out of school. The treatment he received in the
United States became a symbol of AIDS intolerance.

Thankfully, by the late 1980s this ignorant attitude was beginning to subside. Much
admired arts and show business celebrities were being struck down with AIDS, bringing
public attention to the epidemic. Campaigns such as that by the late Diana, Princess of
Wales and a host of famous people worldwide have gradually helped to remove the **stigma**
surrounding AIDS. The Terrence Higgins Trust (named after the first person to die of AIDS in
Britain) conducts educational campaigns which help to correct misunderstandings about the
spread of the virus. The public's fear of AIDS began to turn into shame particularly with the
ways in which some sufferers had been treated as 'outcasts'.

Activities

7 Diana, Princess of Wales made newspaper headlines across the world when she put her arms around an AIDS patient. How do you think this affected people's attitudes towards AIDS and HIV?

8 In pairs discuss what can be done to prevent the spread of HIV and the amount of misinformation about the disease that still circulates among people.

9 You have been asked to promote an AIDS charity that you think the school should support. Prepare a proposal, in the form of an interview, in which you explain the reasons for supporting the charity.

D Marking World AIDS Day – high profile campaigns help to turn the tide in the treatment of AIDS sufferers.

In 1998 the United Nations and World Health Organisation issued a report admitting it had 'grossly underestimated' the scale of the epidemic. Over 30 million people – one in 100 sexually active adults worldwide – were infected with the virus. In addition 16,000 more become infected with HIV every day. The total number of AIDS deaths since the beginning of the epidemic was 11.7 million (including 2.5 million children under the age of 15). The report warned that one in 10 people infected with the virus was unaware of it.

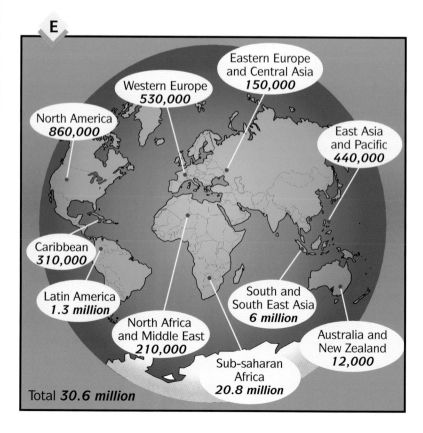

E

Eastern Europe and Central Asia **150,000**

Western Europe **530,000**

North America **860,000**

East Asia and Pacific **440,000**

Caribbean **310,000**

Latin America **1.3 million**

North Africa and Middle East **210,000**

South and South East Asia **6 million**

Australia and New Zealand **12,000**

Sub-saharan Africa **20.8 million**

Total **30.6 million**

AIDS – Pass it on!   **F**

There are two main challenges facing HIV research: to discover a cure for those already infected, and to find a vaccine to prevent anyone else becoming infected. Normally a vaccine contains a weakened or dead form of the infecting organism. The vaccine stimulates the body's immune system to produce antibodies which remember the organism. Then, if the disease attacks the body again, the antibodies recognise and fight it. The danger with AIDS is that the vaccine could destroy the immune system which produces the antibodies in the first place.

There have been advances in finding a cure for those already infected. New three-drug 'cocktails' developed in 1996 have met with some success and are beginning to revolutionise AIDS care. Treatment must start as soon as the patient learns they are infected, before they get ill. The drugs drive the level of HIV in the blood so low that it becomes undetectable. The tablets have to be taken in the right quantities, at the correct intervals otherwise the virus seizes its chance and attacks again. Other drugs are also needed to treat other side-effects of AIDS such as sickness, stomach upsets and skin complaints. It does not, however, work for everyone and the treatment is costly.

There still remains a lot of work to be done in combatting the dangers of HIV/AIDS. Even a few years ago an AIDS diagnosis was a death sentence; now it is a **chronic** condition but it is possible to lead a near-normal life. Better education and medical research is gradually slowing the spread of AIDS in the developed world, but unfortunately it is now increasing in sub-Saharan Africa and South Asia (**E**). Clearly new efforts must be made to target the populations in these areas otherwise the epidemic will continue. Developing countries must be given access to the expensive drugs used to control the action of HIV. Public education and information programmes are essential too. What is vital is cooperation between countries.

THINK ABOUT

1   What is the message behind this cartoon strip (**F**)?

2   Do you think the cartoon is effective in getting the message across?

What do you think ?

'We can't see the end of the epidemic but it is the beginning of a new era.' What hope is there for the future?

Information

Every move you make
Every step you take
I'll be watching you.

('Every Breath You Take' – The Police)

Information: knowledge or something told.

Information is power. It gives the Government a great deal of power if they are the only people who know the full facts.

(BBC Lifeschool programme)

AIM

The unit examines why sometimes the public is not allowed full access to information, and how an individual's right to privacy is not always automatic.

Our right to be left alone has gradually disappeared over the last 30 years. Original government databases of the 1950s were relatively inaccessible. The desktop computer revolution of the 1970s however made previously hidden information much easier to obtain. Computers today are having a major impact on society as they are commonly used for gathering and storing information.

In modern society it is difficult to have secrets. At the cashpoint machines, on the Internet, even when walking down the street people are watching our every move. Whether we like it or not we live in a computer age and consequently, we are all seen as data by thousands of organisations and companies. Information on everything from our credit status to our mental health is easily compiled on databases. Complete personal privacy now appears to be a thing of the past.

IN THE NEWS

THE DEATH OF PRIVACY

Beware the credit card fraud

SECURITY CAMERAS CUT DOWN CRIME

No information is safe

How you are spied on

Activities

1 Who do you think has information about you and your parents?

2 What sort of information about you should be kept strictly confidential?

Invasion of privacy?

In order to claim benefits a person has to give away private details which are then stored on a database. Most people willingly give out their phone numbers and addresses when they are listed in a telephone directory. If someone uses a bank card in a cashpoint machine their whereabouts are registered. If they live in an urban area it is likely that they will be seen somewhere on a surveillance camera. Everytime they purchase by mail order or in big supermarkets their shopping habits will be noted. In return for all these 'invasions of privacy' they benefit from cash when they need it, security and convenient shopping.

Most people accept, to some extent, that zoom-in close circuit television can be very useful in providing information about crime. Surely no one should object to these cameras if they are properly used, and if they do object, is it because they have something to hide? Cameras in city centres have been successful in reducing vandalism and police speed cameras drastically reduce deaths and injuries from speeding motorists. What concerns some people is who has access to the material gathered and for what purpose?

THINK ABOUT

1 Working in pairs, look at the information on these pages and discuss whether you think it is right that, sometimes, information can be kept about us without our knowledge. Can you think of other everyday events where an individual's privacy can be interfered with?

2 Television cameras are now commonly used in shops and city centres. Are there places where they should not be installed? Why? Are there other places where they could be useful?

3 Do you feel the advantages of this type of technology outweigh the disadvantages?

Computer databases containing information about you can be used throughout the world. The result is that, unknown to you, your name can be mistakenly listed as being a bad credit risk or you can be said to be interested in certain products when you are not. There are ways of protecting your privacy: an unlisted telephone number or paying for everything with cash can give you a degree of privacy but life becomes less comfortable and easy.

It is estimated that on average, every adult's name gets passed between two computers about five times a day – normally for credit checking and bank records. Activity at this frequency clearly carries the risk of mistakes, plus there is the extra problem of **computer hacking**, which is a threat to any confidential information. Without anyone knowing, a computer expert can transfer one year's worth of information onto a floppy disc in about 15 to 30 seconds! An investigation by *The Sunday Times* proved how open the system is to abuse. It only took three hours for private investigators to acquire the confidential files of a dozen people from National Health Service (NHS) records. All that was needed were the names, addresses and births of the people involved.

THINK ABOUT

4 *Discuss the following statements:*

a) *'The storage of confidential information on computer is better than paper files.'*

b) *'Access to health records is important to help companies when hiring people or offering life insurance policies.'*

c) *'The information in people's private health records could be abused.'*

Protest groups such as **Liberty** and the **Campaign for Freedom of Information** believe that we should have free access to our own personal records so mistakes can be corrected and damaging information can be removed. Unfortunately, technology continues to outpace the law. In the 1980s Parliament recognised a growing problem as computer information storage became more common. The Data Protection Act was passed in 1985 and went some way to giving individuals the right to:

● know if personal data about them is being held;
● view the data and to correct it if needed.

Are you being spied on?   **B**

How you can be spied on

Bank machines	The location, time and date of each transaction are recorded.
Browsing on the web	What you have been looking at can be recorded.
Employee ID scanners	Magnetic swipe passes into buildings record your whereabouts.
Cellular phone	Your calls can be intercepted and the numbers used easily traced.
Credit cards	Everything charged to you is in a database.
Vote registering	Vote registration records which include your birth date and address are public.

Activities

3 Why do we need a secret service in Britain?

4 List the ways in which information about people can be collected and stored. Which of these methods are for our own protection and which for use by other people?

Many people believe that we need more legal protection to maintain individual privacy. One answer to the privacy question is to have more knowledge about who is watching the public and to whom that information is available.

In Britain, as in many other countries, intelligence agencies are often at work. These organisations serve a twofold purpose:

a) they preserve the nation's security;

b) they find out what others are doing.

In the name of national security individuals can have their phone conversations taped, files containing private information examined and their every move monitored.

Making a phone call	Phone companies can note the number you are calling and who is calling you.
Supermarket scanners	Bonus cards can give information about the sort of things you purchase.
Surveillance cameras	Cameras are widespread – in banks, schools, hospitals and high streets.
Mail order	Many mail order companies sell lists of their customers.
E-mail	Offices regard E-mail as part of your work and employers are entitled to read it if they wish.

The media like a sensational headline intruding into someone's privacy as it is normally good for circulation or audience numbers. Whether the story serves the public interest or not is often doubtful. Newspapers often have no interest in deciding where a private life ends and a public life begins. The crucial element is whether the story is interesting to the public. An individual's feelings have little consideration in the media world.

If someone is **libelled** in the press it is possible, if they are able to pay the costs and prepare for a lengthy court case, to clear their name. Increasingly however some people, especially celebrities, have found themselves victims of 'Web-smear', where unauthorised photos and information can be made freely available on the Internet. Again the law has not caught up with progress. The Web is not so easily sued for libel as a malicious newspaper or magazine article can be.

Basically, the question of information focuses on two kinds of public interest:

a) What is in the interest of the public? (One must accept that the public is interested in a lot of things.)

b) What is it that is happening in the world that people should be interested in?

In this country the general view is that people are told what they need to know. Other countries take a more liberal position, believing that the public have a right to know everything. There are also countries where the people are kept very much in the dark and the media are heavily **censored**

The British press remains bound by our laws on official secrets, confidence and contempt of court. Most people agree that authorities should have the right to suppress material which could be offensive or dangerous to the public good. This power, however, can be open to abuse. In some countries the measures taken to suppress information can be extreme: in Kenya the police disable the printing presses of publications they do not like. On the publication of *The Satanic Verses*, the author, Salman Rushdie, had a death threat (finally withdrawn in 1998) placed on him by the late Ayatollah Khomeni, the religious and spiritual leader of Iran.

Even the right to print information already available to the public can be open to question and has been challenged. In 1986 the courts ruled that the government had been correct to impose an **injunction** on two leading British newspapers. In the interests of national security they were forbidden to print any extracts from the memoirs of Peter Wright, a former MI5 agent. His book, *Spycatcher*, became a bestseller in the United States and people bought copies there and brought them back to Britain. In 1987 the government tried to extend the ban on a third newspaper and this action was challenged under the ruling of Article 10 of the European Convention, which guarantees freedom of information. In lifting the injunction the judges' conclusion was that the government had placed 'the reputation of the security service' before the public's legitimate right to know.

Activity

5 Examine the question, 'Should public figures have a right to privacy?' Prepare a presentation or report on the subject of whether modern technology now allows us to go too far in reporting on the lives of royalty and celebrities.

Without doubt data collection aids the smooth running of government and business and the general availability of data supports freedom of speech and freedom of the press. For many, the new information technologies make life easier but they come at a cost because personal privacy can be lost. A balance is necessary between reckless use of information on the one hand, and total secrecy on the other. It is not so much a question of people having something to hide. They just want some measure of control over what is known about them. Many people believe that new computers gather information so quickly that they have tipped the balance against personal privacy.

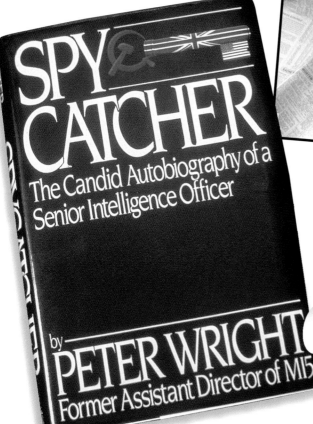

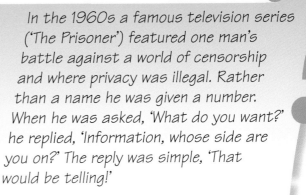
C The heavy hand of censorship: *Spycatcher* and *Lady Chatterley's Lover*.

What do you think

In the 1960s a famous television series ('The Prisoner') featured one man's battle against a world of censorship and where privacy was illegal. Rather than a name he was given a number. When he was asked, 'What do you want?' he replied, 'Information, whose side are you on?' The reply was simple, 'That would be telling!'

Is it fair that governments and organisations have so much information on us and yet we have so little information on them?

Justice

Justice: fairness or the exercise of authority in the maintenance of right.

Justice should not only be done, but should manifestly and undoubtedly be seen to be done.

(Lord Hewart, Law Lord)

*Yet I shall temper...
Justice with mercy.*

(John Milton, Poet)

AIM This unit focuses on the demands of justice and the need for forgiveness and mercy when linked to the concept of punishment.

A central principle of a just society is that everyone is entitled to 'life, liberty and the pursuit of happiness'. Unfortunately, some people abuse this right and as a result face the process of 'justice'. In the past justice seemed quite straightforward. If you committed a crime you were punished either by execution, banishment or fines. Many punishments however were too severe and did not 'fit the crime' (**A**).

The punishment fits the crime!

DORSET
ANY PERSON WILFULLY INJURING
ANY PART OF THIS COUNTY BRIDGE
WILL BE GUILTY OF FELONY AND
UPON CONVICTION LIABLE TO BE
TRANSPORTED FOR LIFE
BY THE COURT
7 & 8 GEO 4 C 30 S 13   T FOOKS

1 *In an interview Mrs Denise Bulger commented: 'Never a day goes by when I don't think of James. But I never think about that awful day, and I rarely think of those murderers – it would kill me if I did. I still have so much hatred for them'.*

Discuss what Mrs Bulger said. What do you think of her view and attitude? Should the views of victims be taken into consideration when deciding the sentence for offenders?

B   The security camera catches a chilling image

In this country, until the nineteenth century, prison was only used on a temporary basis for people awaiting punishment. More prisons were built to accommodate the rising numbers of criminals and many of these buildings are still in use today.

On 13 August 1964 John Welby and Peter Allen made history by becoming the last people to be legally executed in Britain. One year later the death penalty was abolished, although technically it could still be reinstated for certain offences. The last British prison whipping was in 1967, but children were still legally beaten in schools until 1986. New statistics show that Britain faces a rise in violent crimes and many people believe that our present justice system is flawed and appears to be failing.

Throughout the twentieth century we have witnessed a dramatic escalation in crime. Horrific crimes appear to be regularly reported in news items. In 1992 even hardened police officers were shocked at the abduction and subsequent murder of a two year-old boy, Jamie Bulger. For a brief second his mother had let go of his hand in a butcher's shop as she reached for her purse in a bag. The killers were caught on a shopping centre security camera, holding his hand, leading him away to his death (**B**). The nation was shocked at this horrific image and then astonished when the murderers turned out to be two 10 year-old boys.

IN THE NEWS

We demand justice for the victims of crime, not the offenders!

INNOCENT MAN RELEASED AFTER SIXTEEN YEARS IN PRISON

Bring back the short, sharp shock

How can we punish these teenage thugs?

1 What do you think is meant by the 'short sharp shock'?

2 Why do so many boys aged 15 to 18 get involved in crime and why do you think girls commit far fewer crimes than boys?

Let the punishment REALLY fit the crime

When an appalling crime like this happens there is often a public outcry to review the justice system and impose much harsher levels of punishment. In the face of increasing crime rates, consecutive governments promise to come down hard on criminals and yet little seems to change. In particular, present laws seem unable to cope with juvenile crime and many people believe that nowadays the justice system tends to favour the criminal rather than the victim.

Clearly society faces a problem with some of its members who insist on breaking the 'rules'. We must find a way to deal with these law-breakers while at the same time protecting society and the individual. Traditionally there are six main aims of punishment and most sentences handed out to offenders are a mixture of several of these:

Six main aims of punishment

Deterrence
Punishment will discourage the individual from re-offending. It is also hoped that the fear of punishment will put off other potential criminals.

Protection
By locking away someone society is protected from anti-social behaviour.

Retribution
The belief that criminals should be given a punishment that fits the crime.

In Britain more than one in three men has a criminal record by the age of 40, and the prison population is the highest in Western Europe. Whereas America has steadily cut its crime rate in recent years, in England and Wales the number of crimes has doubled since 1979. Reports suggest that British judges are far more ready to imprison offenders than European judges, who want to protect society by reforming criminals through other means such as community service. Also British prisons are some of the most overcrowded and backward in the Developed World. We now accept that, in this country, a prison sentence is the last thing likely to reform a criminal.

A common news story in the media is the evidence of increasing crime and the apparent ineffectiveness of the punishments given by the justice system. However the media can present a false impression. When looking at the punishment debate, it is important to get things into perspective. For example, old people are led to believe that they are the group most at risk in society whereas in reality it is people under the age of 25 years who are most likely to be victims of crime.

A lot of so-called 'minor' offences such as burglaries, criminal damage and shoplifting are committed by people under the age of 17. However the police often find there is little they can actually do with young offenders. Some parents and members of the public think that these sorts of crimes tend to be a phase that a lot of teenagers go through as they grow up. It is seen as an act of rebellion against parents or authority. But the fact remains that theft costs businesses billions of pounds every year.

THINK ABOUT

2 In pairs, look at the six aims of punishment outlined below. Which do you think are the most realistic? Which one(s) do you agree with most?

3 'Prison is not the right place for offenders because it turns them into hardened criminals and does nothing to reform them.' Do you agree with this statement? State your reasons, and consider what other punishments might be better at stopping people re-offending.

Activities

1 In small groups act out a scene where one teenager is being put under pressure by friends to go shoplifting. Take it in turn to be the one being pressurised. Discuss with the rest of the group about how hard or easy you found it to resist the pressure.

2 With a partner, role-play a scene in which a teenager has to confess to one of their parents that they have been shoplifting.

Reform
Punishment stops people from committing more crimes and also helps them to become responsible members of society.

Reparation
Law-breakers must be prepared to make amends either by paying back something to the victim or to society.

Vindication
The laws of society must be respected and be seen to be upheld so people feel safe.

C O J Simpson (above) and Derek Bentley (left). Justice or miscarriage of justice?

HERE LIES
DEREK WILLIAM BENTLEY

A Victim of British Justice

30th June 1933 - 28th January 1953

The media also have a habit of focusing their attention on foreign justice systems. There were several cases abroad during the 1990s which led to extensive coverage in Britain.

In the United States some courtrooms allow television cameras so we are able to follow the proceedings very closely. There was outrage in 1995 when a celebrity ex-sportsman and actor, O J Simpson, was found not guilty of the murder of his ex-wife and her friend. American and British newspapers carried headlines that justice in the United States was a 'joke'. In 1997 there was a public outcry in Britain when a court in Boston, USA, found a British nanny guilty of murder. Under pressure the judge changed the jury's verdict and released her. Earlier that year British newspapers were demanding justice and a reversal of the 'barbaric judgement' on two British nurses who were found guilty of murder in Saudi Arabia.

It is fair to say that Britain is not well placed to criticise the practices of other countries. For one particular family, 1998 finally saw justice being done. Derek Bentley was hanged in 1953 for the murder of a policeman during a bungled robbery. The Bentley family always maintained that he should never have been executed for his part in the killing of PC Miles. The policeman was shot dead by Bentley's accomplice, 16 year-old Christopher Craig. At the time of the killing, Bentley was already under arrest and was being led away by police officers. At his trial, Lord Chief Justice Goddard told the jury that when two people were involved in a criminal activity which ends in murder, both were guilty in law, whoever fired the shots. Derek Bentley was executed while Christopher Craig was eventually released and now leads a normal life. In 1998 the case was referred back to the Court of Appeal where Bentley was given a full **posthumous** pardon.

D Injustice!

This execution, as well as several other famous 'miscarriages of justice' led to the abolition of the death penalty in Britain in 1965. The punishment of offenders in Britain, however, is still much criticised. When the Criminal Cases Review Commission was set up in 1997, Derek Bentley was just one of 892 cases that the Commission was asked to investigate.

If justice is not seen to be done the results can be severe. In 1991 during an incident relating to a traffic offence, four Los Angeles policemen savagely beat up Rodney King, a black motorist. The whole incident was videotaped by a bystander. In 1992 the policemen were found not guilty of assault by a jury which included no black members. After the verdict, whole districts of the city of Los Angeles erupted into two days of rioting, arson, murder and looting leaving at least 58 dead and thousands injured (**D**).

Most people accept that punishment has to be given to those who refuse to abide by society's rules. The aims of revenge and retaliation, however, are not justifiable. The key aims should be reform and protection, and punishment must distinguish between the demands of justice and the need for forgiveness. Justice is about sorting the innocent from the guilty. If you do not have a fair trial you have what is really just a punishment system. If this causes innocent people to be in danger of punishment, there is no real justice.

What do you think ?

In your opinion, can a system that causes innocent people to be in danger of punishment be described as 'justice'?

Kill

Kill: to cause or bring about death.

The law should not be changed and the deliberate taking of human life should remain a crime.

(The British Medical Association, 1988)

Many of us find moral problems about killing difficult, and most of us who do not should do.

(Jonathan Glover, Philosopher)

AIM This unit examines whether it is morally justifiable to override a person's right to live or die.

Attitudes to killing and death vary from society to society. In Ancient Greece, for example, it was thought perfectly acceptable to kill any newborn babies that were deformed. Suicide was generally seen as a coward's way of avoiding life's problems, but was an honourable alternative if a person had an incurable disease and faced a lingering, painful death. The Romans argued that suicide was a perfectly acceptable option whenever a person decided that life was no longer desirable.

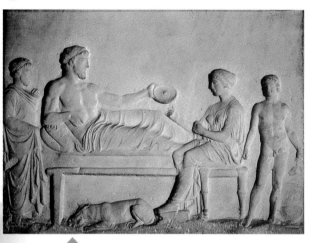

A A relief from the fourth century BC. When he was charged with corruption and sentenced to death by public stoning, the Greek philosopher Socrates was handed a poison to allow him to commit suicide.

Christianity brought a change in these viewpoints. The first Christians were pacifists and opposed to killing in almost all circumstances. War, capital punishment, suicide, euthanasia and abortion were all condemned practices. However, opposition to war and capital punishment was soon lifted because the early Church leaders felt that Christianity could not oppose war and expect to become a state religion.

These sorts of developments are still evident in the way modern societies think and behave. There is respect for life but one question still remains – under what circumstances, if any, is it right to destroy a human life? In some circumstances killing in war and capital punishment may be permissible. Suicide is no longer regarded as a criminal offence. There is, unfortunately, a great deal of confusion and anxiety over our attitude to the **sanctity** of life and nowhere more so than in the field of medicine.

Advances in medical technology have saved lives and eased suffering for thousands of patients, but modern methods now enable very sick or injured people, who would otherwise have died, to live possibly for years, sometimes with no meaningful quality of life. This has led to debate about the medical profession's commitment to saving life or destroying it. The issues of abortion, euthanasia and embryo experimentation have caused intense controversy and forced us to re-examine what should be permitted or banned by law.

IN THE NEWS

Embryos to be used as 'spare parts'

Euthanasia doctor accused of executions

To die with dignity

Who lives, who dies, who chooses?

ABORTION ROW FATHER TAKES BATTLE TO THE COURTS

1 What problems do you think modern advances in medicine have brought about?

2 What do you think could be the situation behind the headline 'Who lives, who dies, who chooses'?

3 Suicide has been described as the 'most selfish of acts'. Do you agree? Why have attitudes towards suicide changed over the last 30 years?

Euthanasia

The term comes from the Greek language: eu meaning 'good' and thanatos meaning 'death'. It now refers to the act of ending another person's life, at their request, by painless means in order to minimise suffering – in other words, 'mercy killing'.

Euthanasia comes in two main forms, **passive** and **active**. Legally the former is acceptable whereas the latter is regarded as murder.

- Passive – allowing a patient to die by withholding medical treatment.
- Active – taking a direct action designed to kill the patient.

A further distinction is often made between **voluntary** and **non-voluntary** euthanasia. The former term occurs when a person has expressed a wish to be allowed to die. The latter term applies to individuals who are in comas from which they will not recover and so cannot express an opinion. These people are described by doctors as being in a Persistent Vegetative State (PVS).

Many arguments, some for and some against, are raised by the issue of euthanasia (see box on right).

Despite pressure to change the present laws, active euthanasia in Britain is a crime carrying a possible prison sentence for the individual who performs it. There have, however, been several high-profile cases involving terminally ill patients requesting medical assistance in committing suicide. In the vast majority of these cases the accused individuals have been let off by the courts.

- Many terminally ill patients are in great pain and/or experience a poor quality of life.
- If someone faces life with a painful and incurable disease and wants to die, there is little difference between taking their own life (suicide) or asking someone to help them die (euthanasia).
- Is it right to use limited resources on expensive treatment merely to prolong the life of a dying person by a few days or weeks?
- If euthanasia was openly practised, some patients would fear their doctors rather than trust them.
- Many faith groups believe that suffering can have a positive value for the terminally ill and for the carers.
- Some argue that pain can be controlled to tolerable levels by the use of drugs.
- By making euthanasia available some people could be pressured or influenced by others.
- If animals are suffering we do not hesitate to have them put down so why not humans?
- Some people who make the request are clinically depressed.

Activities

1 Set out the arguments listed on page 65 under two columns headed 'For' and 'Against'. What do you think are the main dangers of making euthanasia lawful?

2 What is the main difference between voluntary and non-voluntary euthanasia?

3 Is there any difference between killing someone and intentionally failing to save their life?

4 Should doctors have to use every means available to preserve life if there is no possibility of a reasonable 'quality of life' for the patient?

CASE STUDIES

A
Dr Nigel Cox administered a fatal dose of potassium chloride to his elderly patient, Mrs Lilian Boyes. She was close to death and in great pain. After consulting her two sons, she asked Dr Cox to help her die painlessly which he did. The doctor noted the injection in the medical records, making no effort to conceal what he had done.

Accused of attempted murder – court verdict: a suspended prison sentence and allowed to continue his work.

B
Andrew and Nicola Thompson tried to administer a potentially fatal overdose of a powerful pain killer after their terminally ill mother begged them to end her suffering. They immediately told hospital staff what they had done and the mother was brought back from the brink of death only to die in terrible pain 12 days later.

Accused of attempted murder – court verdict: conditional discharge.

Generally, the governments of most countries appear to avoid dealing with the issue. No country has legalised active euthanasia but some have a more positive attitude to it. In Japan the courts have listed four conditions under which mercy killing is permitted:

1 The patient is suffering unbearable physical pain.
2 Death is imminent and inevitable.
3 All efforts have been made to eliminate the pain.
4 The patient wishes to have their life ended.

Euthanasia is illegal in Holland but a law was passed in 1993 which prevents doctors from being prosecuted as long as they follow certain procedures. The same four conditions set out by the Japanese courts are upheld and two further conditions are also necessary:

1 Two doctors agree on the procedure.
2 Relatives are consulted.

The Voluntary Euthanasia Society (EXIT) argues that anyone suffering from a useless and painful existence should have the right to die under their own terms. The society argues for a set of safeguards, like those used in Japan and Holland, to ensure that the procedure is not abused. Strict controls are needed to ensure that a patient is not influenced by others and that they are of 'sound mind' when they make the request. The society believes that this can be achieved if the patient has made a 'living will', stating how they want to be treated.

THINK ABOUT

1 Should we have the right to choose to end our lives when we wish?

2 In groups, look at the two case studies and discuss the verdicts that were given.

Abortion

The word comes from the Latin word aboriri, meaning 'to fail to be born'. Medically the term describes the destruction of life after conception and before birth. In 1861 The Offences Against the Person Act was passed to reduce the number of deaths from 'back-street' (illegal) abortions. The Act made it illegal to 'procure a miscarriage'.

These dangerous 'back-street' operations continued however and in the 1930s a campaign began to legalise abortion. In 1938 Dr Aleck Bourne invited police to prosecute him for carrying out an abortion on a 14 year-old rape victim. He was let off on the grounds that he acted to save her life. By the 1960s legal abortion could be obtained by people who could afford to 'buy' a surgeon and two psychiatrists to testify that the pregnant woman's mental health would be in danger if she went through with the pregnancy. Another alternative was to travel to a country where abortion was legal and pay to have the operation. However, those seeking reform of the abortion law accepted that these two options were not available to very poor people. It is estimated that over 100,000 illegal operations were performed each year in the early 1960s. There were at least 12 reported deaths and many women suffered infertility or illness as a result.

A further important factor which influenced people's opinions about abortion was the Thalidomide drug, originally prescribed to women early on in pregnancy to avoid sickness. In the early 1960s the public began to witness the terrible side-effects of the drug as babies were born with awful physical deformities. Steadfast campaigning by groups such as the Abortion Law Reform Society ensured that there was a public demand for change in the abortion laws.

Eventually, in October 1967 the Abortion Act came into force which set out a framework for legal abortions.

Contrary to popular belief, no time limit was set but under normal circumstances the pregnancy should not have passed the 28th week.

ABORTION ACT 1967

An abortion may be performed legally if two or more doctors certify that:

1 the mental or physical health of the woman or her existing children will suffer if the pregnancy continues, or

2 the child, if born, would be seriously physically or mentally handicapped.

5 Set out the reasons why you think the 1967 Abortion Act was necessary. In your opinion, do you think the two conditions for abortion went far enough?

B Photos of foetuses still play a part in the abortion debate

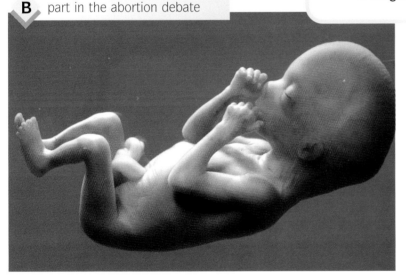

THINK ABOUT

3 *Why do you think photos like **B** are used by opponents of abortion?*

4 *'It is a woman's right to choose whether to have an abortion or not.' Discuss your views on abortion and in pairs produce a statement which summarises the different points of view about the woman's right to choose. Read the arguments for and against abortion on page 68 and select one from each side which you both feel is the most powerful.*

From April 1991 the law on abortion was changed as the Human Fertilisation and Embryology Act became law. This amended the 1967 Act by inserting a 24 week limit for abortion. The operation is still permitted after 24 weeks if the pregnancy involves risk to the life of the woman or in the case of the foetus being seriously handicapped.

Today groups such as Life and SPUC (Society for the Protection of the Unborn Child) oppose abortion. Medical advances mean that foetal operations can now be performed on deformities that previously would have led to abortions. One lobby argues strongly that aborting malformed foetuses is discrimination against disabled people.

Opinions remain divided over abortion. Some people believe that the choice should rest solely with the pregnant woman whereas others argue that the deliberate killing of unborn human life is always wrong. Some believe that abortion is permissible in the case of rape but debatable when the woman has chosen to be in a sexual relationship.

Without doubt the arguments for and against abortion are powerful and persuasive.

Abortion – life in the balance

For abortion (pro-choice)

- Women should have the right to choose what happens to their bodies.
- The mother's life or her physical/mental health is at risk.
- It is irresponsible to have an unwanted child.
- Tests reveal an abnormality of the foetus that will drastically impair the quality of its life.
- The mother is HIV-positive.
- The pregnancy is a result of a sexual crime.
- The mother is very young or physically or emotionally immature.
- The quality of life for the rest of the family will be drastically reduced.

Against abortion (pro-life)

- No one has the right to take a life and the foetus is a potential human being.
- The rights of the unborn child are equal to those of the mother.
- If abortions are allowed the 'sanctity of life' principle could become increasingly weakened.
- Late abortion operations can be dangerous and use up hospital resources that could help others.
- The effects of abortion can cause the mother emotional distress and create health problems in the future.
- Doctors and nurses feel that the saving of human life is more satisfying than destroying it.
- When there are contraceptives freely available, abortion should not be used as a 'last resort' birth control.
- Physically or mentally handicapped individuals can lead full and rewarding lives.

 C The continuing war of words…

Embryo experimentation

The experimentation on and destruction of embryos created by **in vitro fertilisation (IVF)** are now causing further ethical problems about when, if ever, killing is justified. In vitro simply means 'in glass', and IVF is the fertilisation of egg and sperm outside of the body – in a glass petri dish.

In 1978 Louise Brown, the world's first test-tube baby was born following this method. The medical technique of in vitro fertilisation is now commonplace but controversy still surrounds it. With IVF treatment, normally the woman uses drugs to stimulate egg production. Eggs are then extracted and a number are fertilised. Two days after fertilisation, the embryo or pre-embryo has developed to about eight cells and is then placed in the woman's uterus. Implantation appears to work best if several embryos are placed in the uterus. Generally one embryo will implant and the others are discharged from the woman's body, but occasionally more than one embryo implants and multiple births result. To reduce the danger to the mother, selective reduction is sometimes practised

Activity

6 Write or role-play a scene where a teenage girl, who is pregnant, discusses with a doctor the options open to her.

by injecting potassium chloride into one or more of the developing foetuses. Faulty embryos are destroyed and any embryos not implanted will either be frozen or discarded. Many people believe that these procedures involve the killing of human life.

Activities

7 What does IVF stand for?

8 With IVF treatment, why are several embryos created rather than just one?

9 A lot of people believe that having a child is a gift not a right. What do you think?

10 Should medical research make it possible for a couple to have a child if they want one?

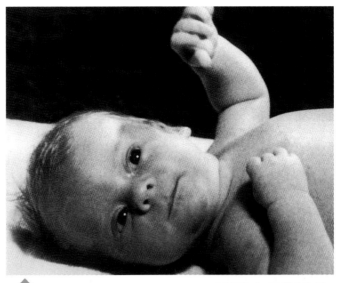

 D Louise Brown – the first baby conceived in a petri dish

Frozen sperm **E**

The frozen 'spare embryos' can be used if the first attempt at implantation fails. Some of these embryos, however, are used for experiments. A further issue arises from experimentation with the spare embryos created in the laboratory. Many scientists insist that this research is essential in order to perfect in vitro techniques and research into genetic diseases. Already, tissue from aborted foetuses is being used to treat adults and the suggestion is being made that frozen embryos could be used for 'spare parts'. Some people believe that life is being created and then deliberately destroyed. IVF techniques are seen to be creating new demands and new problems rather than treating infertility which should be its function.

THINK ABOUT

5 'Experimentation on human embryos should be banned.' Discuss the arguments for and against this comment. If working in a group say which arguments you agree or diagree with and why.

There is an interesting link between the issues of euthanasia, abortion and embryo experimentation. In all of them doctors are accused by some groups of killing human or potential human beings. Just as the state has legalised certain acts of killing such as war and capital punishment, it appears that the medical world now also has the right to do the same.

What do you think ?

Should the medical world's concern be to preserve life at all costs or should the 'quality of life' be the main consideration?

Love

> You know very well that love is, above all, the gift of oneself.
>
> (Jean Anouilh, Playwright)

Love: an intense feeling of deep affection or great liking for a person or thing.

> Love built on beauty, soon as beauty, dies.
>
> (John Donne, Poet)

AIM The unit looks at the many meanings of the word 'love' and how people cope with personal relationships.

In the past the perfect relationship consisted of love, marriage and sex in that order. A person meets someone, falls in love and lives happily ever after. In modern society, however, marriage sometimes now comes last on the list of three. The fact that two in every five marriages will end in divorce seems to suggest that the concept of the 'ideal relationship' is false.

The look of love! **A**

Activities

'I love you.'

'I love swimming.'

'I love my pet cat.'

'I love eating out.'

'I love my father.'

1 Are all these 'love'?

2 Write the word LOVE and then note down the first five words or phrases that come into your mind when you think of the word love.

3 Finish this sentence in three different ways: 'Love is…'

Although many people still seek stability through marriage and family, they appear to expect too much from marriage. The media portray the ideal picture of a beautiful house, lots of money and perfect children. The reality is different. If the marriage fails divorce is an easy option. Arguments, relationship breakdowns and divorce bring many problems, some of which may remain with the individuals concerned for life.

THINK ABOUT

1 Discuss the following questions in small groups. Someone in the group should note down the different views put forward by members of the group.

   a) Is it possible to love more than one person at a time?
   b) What is the difference between loving someone and being in love with them?
   c) In what ways can love hurt?
   d) What does 'being loved' mean to you?

2 Make a list of six things you hope for in a lasting relationship.

IN THE NEWS

Love hurts!

EXPECTATIONS IN MARRIAGE ARE TOO HIGH

Divorce rates continue to rise

The price of love

I want to know what love is!

B Mail order love?

Historically in Britain love was not seen as necessary for couples and 'arranged' marriages were quite normal. In many parts of the world arranged marriages are still practised today and are based on shared values rather than romance. Love is seen as important but it may develop after marriage, not necessarily before. Quite often choices in arranged or assisted marriages are influenced by considerations of economic security, family background and professional status. The importance placed upon romantic love varies between cultures. In western cultures today, love generally precedes marriage; in others, it more often follows marriage.

A new trend in relationships has recently emerged as men and women use dating or introduction agencies. Their adverts can often be found in women's and men's magazines. Now with the Internet

WELCOME TO ROMANTIC LINKS PAGE!

This site provides links to the best romantic resources on the Web - matchmaking, dating, mail-order, special interests etc. Please feel free to click around, and, who knows, maybe you will find that special one you've been looking for!

My name is Elza. I am from Russia. I am 25. I want to have a happy family, to give all my love to my husband and children. TO FIND OUT MORE, CLICK HERE! ●

please visit our sponsor

Please click one of these links to be taken directly to a specific section:

| National | International | Matchmaking | Special interests | Add URL |

Aarens Dating Directory — Featured Site

Visit Dream Date Superlinks

Lonehart Surf Site

Singles Stop — A Designated Single's Stop

CNI — A Cupid's Network Affiliate

SingleSites.com — A SingleSites.com Destination

★★★★ *Romance Links* — A 4^ Romance Links Affiliate

○ A singles place — Where singles meet

THINK ABOUT

3 In some traditions, marriages are 'arranged'. Do you think this is a good idea?

4 Why do some people object to arranged marriages?

5 What are the advantages and disadvantages of using dating agencies to meet a partner?

Four definitions of love

Agape
a purely selfless love. Showing concern for the well-being of others, it involves charity, tolerance and respect for all people.

Eros
a love based on sexual passion/affection. It is based on the physical attraction that people have for one another, the state of 'falling in love'.

Storge
the love and affection we have towards certain things or places.

Philos
the kind of love expressed in friendships and those close to us such as relatives.

these agencies even extend internationally as individuals look for love overseas and go in search of their ideal partner.

One of the problems with the word 'love' is that it is used so often that it has many meanings. For example, there is a great deal of confusion between love and sex. To many people 'making love' is just another term for having sex. The word love usually refers to the whole relationship between a couple, including sex. And when we speak about love or loving we clearly do not always mean the same thing. Loving our parents is a different feeling than the love we show towards a pet or our love of a particular food. Love is not a straightforward emotion.

Some languages have different words to describe different kinds of love. Hindus have 20 different words in Sanskrit which describe love and the Greek language makes use of four different words to denote types of love (**C**).

The love that leads to marriage does not mean love in the sense of liking things. It is also quite different from the friendship and affection which must be present in a marriage. These kinds of love are different from the love we refer to when we say that we have 'fallen in love'. This is not easy to describe. It is a desire to be completely united with another person. Even amongst the most secure of relationships, we accept that arguments occur and difficulties can arise but the individuals continue to love each other.

People sometimes get very confused by the emotions connected with love. A normal part of growing up is to be infatuated or to 'have a crush' on someone. Sometimes this can be with a person they have never met such as a film or pop star. Unfortunately, for some individuals this feeling does not fade and can develop into a dangerous obsession. Some go to great lengths to convince the other person of their 'love', sending presents, following them home and telephoning at all hours of the day and night. Several high profile cases have featured celebrities who became targets for disturbed fans. This behaviour becomes destructive and in extreme cases it is now recognised as the crime of **stalking**. A law was introduced to protect people whose lives were made miserable by this obsessive behaviour.

In a healthy relationship there are elements that appear to be common to all loving relationships whether between husband and wife or best friends:

a) mutual understanding;
b) giving and receiving support;
c) valuing and enjoying being with the loved one.

The **psychologist** Robert Sternberg views love as a triangle, whose three points are passion, intimacy and commitment (**D**). As far as Sternberg is concerned consummate love is the ideal, the love which all relationships should be based on.

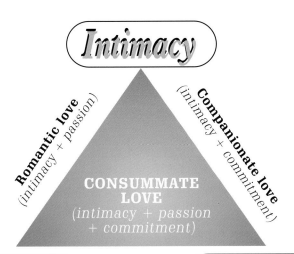

The love triangle – the three basic components of love **D**

The longer a relationship lasts, the fewer its emotional ups and downs. No high lasts forever and as a relationship develops over years, inevitably passion cools and other factors such as shared values become increasingly important. The steadier companionate love develops, a level which is more low key but it is rooted in deep affectionate links.

Activities

4 What is the difference between liking and loving?

5 Which four words do the Greeks use for love? What do they mean by them?

6 Write down the main things you would hope for in a romantic relationship. Do you think a boy expects different things from a relationship than a girl?

7 Letters pages in many magazines are full of worries about love and sex. Working in pairs or groups, look at the problem pages of three or four magazines. Do you think the situations are realistic? What do you think of the advice given?

8 Select one of the letters and act out a discussion in which several 'experts' explain how they would respond to the letter.

What do you think

'I thought I knew what love was
What did I know?
Those days are gone forever
I should just let them go.'

(Don Henley – The Boys of Summer)

Are our expectations of love too high?

Media

Media: a word used to cover different forms of communication (such as newspapers, television, radio and the internet) that reach large numbers of people.

The media are all around us. In many cases we do not realise how much we use them, or how much, and in what ways, they influence us.

(Iain Hughes, Author)

One picture is worth ten thousand words.

(Frederick Barnard)

AIM The unit examines the ways in which the media in all their many forms have an impact on our everyday lives.

Today we can send documents across the world in a matter of seconds, or easily telephone someone thousands of miles away. A news item will flash onto our TV screens almost as soon as it happens. Communication through the media in the 1990s is immediate.

The word 'media' is very much an invention of the twentieth century. In the last century the press was the main means of communication to the educated masses. In the late nineteenth century photography became a new method of passing on information to a large audience. In the 1920s radio and later television increased the size of the potential audience still further and the term 'media' was used to describe the information industry. In the western world, newspapers, magazines and the cinema are no longer the main forms of media, but they are still important.

THINK ABOUT

Look at the pictures (A). List all the types of media which you can recognise. Which one is:
a) the most influential?
b) the one you use least?
c) the most recent?

Give reasons for your answers.

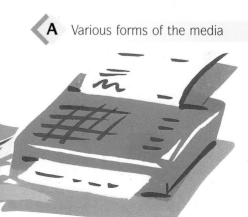

A Various forms of the media

Date	Event
17th/18th century	Newspapers first printed.
1785	First newspaper, *The Spectator* (later became *The Times*) published.
Early 1800s	Newspaper production is speeded up by the introduction of steam powered printing presses.
1840	The English scientist W H Fox Talbot invents the first positive-negative camera.
1845	The first public telegraph line is opened in the USA. The message is transmitted by electric current in the 'dash-dot' code developed by Samuel Morse.
1876	Scots-born scientist Alexander Graham Bell sends the first long distance message by voice using his invention – the telephone.
1877	Thomas Edison invents sound recording.
1895	The French brothers Louis and Auguste Lumière open the world's first cinema in Paris. They use the projector/camera they developed from a camera/cine viewer designed in the 1880s by Thomas Edison.
	Guglielmo Marconi transmits the first radio signals.
	The radio age begins in 1901 when he sends a morse code signal across the Atlantic.
Early 20th century	Cinema gaining in popularity.
1925–26	Scotsman John Logie Baird demonstrates his television system by making the first long distance transmission of a moving picture.
1926	'Talking' films appear.
	British Broadcasting Corporation is set up.
1927	BBC radio established.
1928	Baird demonstrates colour television.
1936	BBC begins the world's first public television service.
1955	Commercial TV begins.
1964	BBC2 on air.
1969	Colour TV is widely available to the public.
1970s	The Internet began as ARPANET, a US military network, and over the following two decades is gradually linked into educational and research organisations.
1972	Commercial radio began.
1977	Teletext introduced.
1982	Introduction of Channel 4.
1985–89	Cable and Satellite TV are developed.
1997	Channel 5 on the air.
1998	Digital television is developed

B Development of the media

C Pioneers of the media world: Alexander Graham Bell (top) and Guglielmo Marconi (below).

Activities

1 Look at the table (**B**) setting out the development of the media. Which type of media was the first to appear? Which type of media was the last to appear? In your opinion, which development was the most important?

2 Using **B**, trace the inventions which led to the development of radio by the use of a flow diagram.

INFORMS   INFLUENCES

MEDIA

EDUCATES   ENTERTAINS

The four main functions **D**

The modern media, both printed and electronic, play an important part in our lives. Not only do they keep us informed, they keep us entertained and exert enormous influence over what we are allowed to know and feel. Quite often we do not appreciate how much we are influenced by them, how powerful they are, and what effects they have on our lives.

Generally all forms of the media serve one or more of four functions (**D**).

Many people think that some things are best left uncommunicated. The media can come under fierce scrutiny if they examine distressing topics, matters of state security or intrude into the private lives of prominent people. The major criticisms are that the media are biased, they create and use **stereotypes** and the media does not show a true picture of society.

IN THE NEWS

We know all about you!

The Internet – marvel or menace?

IS TV THE TERRIBLE TOY IN THE CORNER?

THE KILLING SCREENS

THE POWER OF THE PRESS

1 Consider each of the five headlines. List the positive and the negative aspects of each.

2 Role-play a discussion between an individual who thinks that all forms of the media are good and a person who believes that the media are too powerful. Use the headlines as starter points and refer to the notes that you made in your answer to question one.

Activities

3 In what ways can the media influence people?

4 In this day and age which main function of the media is the most important?

5 Compare a serious (broadsheet) and a popular (tabloid) newspaper. On the same day, how do they differ in their coverage of:
a) headline stories;
b) foreign news;
c) 'showbiz' and sport.

6 Can you find any evidence of **bias** in the way the papers report stories?

 One Levi campaign led to an 800% increase in sales. The company could not keep up with the demand so the advert was withdrawn!

Although the media are regarded with suspicion there is also a strong belief that the public has a right to know about anything that concerns it. The media are the channels for informing the public and therefore serve a crucial role in a free society.

All forms of the mass media can quickly reach huge audiences. It is this ability which gives them their great power, a power that is enhanced because they are able to present easily understood and attractive imagery. Almost daily we come into contact with one of these forms of media. In fact, it is estimated that people spend almost one third of their waking time making use of some part of the media. Consequently, the television, internet, radio and the press are extremely effective in altering people's attitudes, lifestyles, political and moral values.

Companies are well aware of the power of the media and every year spend millions of pounds on advertising. The media seeks to influence us by promoting various goods, drawing our attention to them and encouraging us to buy them. Advertising is expensive but is an important source of media funding, and a successful advertising campaign can drastically boost sales of a product. Levi Strauss, for example, produced a series of 'catchy' adverts that led to a massive increase in demand for their jeans (**E**).

Sometimes the media can influence people without them even being aware of it. History has plenty of examples of how the media can be manipulated and used to stir up emotions and sometimes hatred towards groups of people, and this shows us how powerful they can be.

What do you think

'Today, it seems that we are unable to think for ourselves. The media are part of everyone's life and shape our views of the world.' Is this a fair comment about the effects of the media?

Nuclear

Even if you take into account the effect of Chernobyl there will be less people seriously affected by nuclear power than any other major form of power generation in the world.

(Douglas McRoberts, spokesperson for Nuclear Electrics)

Nuclear energy: energy produced by a nuclear reaction. Nuclear power is the power generated by using this energy to produce steam to drive an electricity generator in a power station.

Environmentalists claim that renewable energy and energy efficiency together are our best hope to meet future energy needs.

(Greenpeace Environmental Trust)

AIM In examining the controversy surrounding nuclear power the unit looks at some of the competing claims for and against it.

The images that most people have of nuclear fission at its most powerful are the atomic explosions over the Japanese cities of Hiroshima and Nagasaki in August 1945. When an atom is split, a large amount of energy is released and this can be used for atomic explosions or to generate electricity. British scientists began research into generating electricity after 1945 and nuclear power stations began operating in 1956.

A Demonstrators against nuclear energy

Nuclear power today is a controversial subject. Some people believe it is the great hope for the future; others insist it will destroy the planet. Those in favour point out that it is cheap, clean and affects far less people than any other power generation in the world. Also, burning **fossil fuels** uses up limited resources and creates an unwanted by-product – carbon dioxide, the major greenhouse gas. Air pollution, acid rain, oil spills and oil rig fires are just some of the environmental and social problems associated with the use of coal, gas and oil. In contrast, nuclear power is 'clean' as it does not contribute to the greenhouse effect or acid rain.

However opponents to nuclear power have been warning of the potential danger of accidents and the damage to the environment. Public confidence in nuclear energy has been reduced by the near catastrophic results from three nuclear disasters:

- Windscale (now renamed Sellafield).
- Three Mile Island.
- Chernobyl.

One major nuclear disaster: Chernobyl

Windscale (Sellafield)

A fire in the nuclear reactor at Windscale in 1957 led to the roads on the west coast of Cumbria being closed, nearby farms cutting back on work and two million gallons of milk having to be destroyed. Houses near the plant were not evacuated and the public was told nothing until the scare was 'over'. These precautions were clearly inadequate: people were exposed to ten times the safe level of radiation. Although there is no proven link with Windscale and cancer, independent medical scientists believe that the leak is likely to have caused 250 to 1,000 cases of thyroid cancer.

Three Mile Island

In 1979, at the American Three Mile Island nuclear reactor, an emergency cooling valve jammed but a control panel light signalled that it was closed. Regarding the warning system as foolproof staff turned off an emergency pump which could have cooled the reactor.

Radiation inside the building reached levels 75 times above those required to kill a human. Radioactive gases poured into the atmosphere and it took days for evacuation and emergency plans to be put into operation. The government was accused of covering up the problem. One billion dollars were spent and yet 11 years later the clean-up operation was still unfinished. Cancer deaths and infant mortality in the area are many times the national average.

Chernobyl

The worst ever nuclear accident occurred at Chernobyl (Russia) on 25 April 1986. Workers broke strict rules by putting the reactor on low power and switching off some safety systems. This resulted in the reactor becoming very unstable and in four seconds it produced 100 times the normal energy and this caused an explosion. Thirty five firemen and plant workers were killed and an area of 50,000 km around the plant was evacuated. The Russian authorities were slow to admit the seriousness of the accident or to realise the worldwide consequences.

The nuclear fall-out which reached 20 countries, including Britain over 1,400 miles away, highlights the gravity of the accident. Five years later, 738 British farms were still affected by fall-out and were restricted in the selling of sheep which had grazed on contaminated land. The most conservative estimates put a figure of 11,000 people contracting cancer as a result of the Chernobyl disaster. Other experts suggest a number ten times higher than that. Millions have undoubtedly had their health damaged since even small levels of radiation exposure can weaken the body's immune system.

The Chernobyl accident caused a crisis of confidence in the world's nuclear industry and led to anti-nuclear demonstrations in several European countries. Today, many people are convinced there is no such thing as a safe nuclear reactor.

Once seen as the answer to global energy problems, the attitude to nuclear power has changed because of the problem of nuclear waste. Near most nuclear power stations levels of radiation can be higher than normal, often representing a gradual build up of waste. Radioactive substances are classified by their 'half life' – the amount of time it takes for half their radioactivity to fade. Nuclear fuel makes use of plutonium with a half life of 24,000 years and uranium which has a half life of 4.5 million years!

Activities

1 Consider what might happen if an accident like Chernobyl happened in your area. Write an article describing an imaginary accident based on your thoughts.

2 In pairs role-play an interview between a reporter and a survivor of a nuclear accident. Take it in turns to be the survivor. Write down your impressions and discuss these with the class.

The safe disposal of nuclear waste is now the subject of much debate. There are three categories of nuclear waste – low, intermediate and high level:

Low level

About 90% of waste is low grade (paper, plastic sheeting and protective clothing) but is still radioactive. None of this waste has a half life of over 30 years and some of it can be disposed of quite safely.

Intermediate level

This includes various parts of nuclear reactors such as cladding and filters. The plants are designed to deal with this waste but it can retain its radioactivity for many centuries. So it has to be disposed of in a way which isolates it from the environment.

High level

High level is spent nuclear fuel. Some products remain radioactive for millions of years and generate heat. They can be converted to glass blocks by a process called 'vitrification' which can be safely managed. The safe storage of this waste at the Sellafield plant is the cause of much controversy.

Some dumping of nuclear waste is allowed but is carefully monitored by British Nuclear Fuels and government scientists. Sellafield for example discharges two million gallons of low level radioactive water every day into the Irish Sea, making it the most radioactively contaminated sea in the world.

It has been estimated that over a 33 year period (1949–82) Britain dumped nearly 75,000 tons of nuclear waste into the North Atlantic, rightly earning its title as 'The Dirty Man of Europe'. In 1997 the decision was taken to stop the dumping of waste at sea and a commitment was made that polluting the sea should be stopped almost entirely by 2020.

THINK ABOUT

1 Why is waste disposal such a problem in the world today?

2 What kinds of waste are people most concerned about?

3 In Britain many local authorities ask householders to sort out their waste before putting it out for collection. Do you think this is a good idea? Are people happy to do this?

4 Nearly 150 years ago a Native American, Chief Seattle, commented:
   'Continue to contaminate your bed, and you will one night suffocate in your own waste.'
   What do you think he meant?

IN THE NEWS

The greenhouse impact of traditional fuels

UK tops nuclear dumping league

A fall-out among friends

Nuclear power – the 'clean' power of the future

Nuclear is safer than the traditional forms of energy!

1 In small groups look through the five headlines and select three which could be described as pro-nuclear.

2 Design a newspaper headline that weighs up the arguments both for and against. For example, 'Greenhouse or fall-out? Your choice!'

As radioactive waste takes thousands of years to decay, some plans for its disposal suggested putting high and intermediate level waste miles underground sealed in concrete. Environmental groups such as Greenpeace, Friends of the Earth and CND (Campaign for Nuclear Disarmament) believe that storage must be above ground so we can act in case there are any leaks. No method of disposal has been proved to work for the thousands of years necessary before the waste becomes safe. In addition to leaks, governments must also take into account potential dangers such as terrorists, earthquakes and even ice ages.

Around some nuclear reactor sites in Britain medical researchers have discovered much higher incidents than the national average of childhood **leukaemia**. The media have been quick to try to directly link this illness to the power plants but actual proof is difficult to find. However the implications are still very disturbing and there are frequent calls for more research. Many people fear radiation, associating it with the fall-out of atomic bombs or disasters such as Chernobyl or Three Mile Island.

What must be remembered is that everyone, no matter where they live, is exposed to 'background' radiation from natural sources. Scientists estimate that a person living in Britain receives an average annual dose of 1.87 millisieverts (mSv) from natural sources. This represents about 87% of the total annual dose of 2.142 mSv, the remaining 13% coming from man-made processes.

Cosmic rays (0.3 mSv)

Ground and buildings (0.4 mSv)

Drink (0.37 mSv)

Natural radioactivity in the air (0.8 mSv)

SOURCE OF RADIATION

Fall-out from nuclear weapons (0.01 mSv)

Air travel (0.01 mSv)

Medical (0.25 mSv)

Nuclear power (0.002 mSv)

Sources of radiation in Britain C

3 A proposal has been made to build a nuclear processing plant in your area. In small groups make a list of those people who would probably be in favour of the site and those who would be against it. Within the group allocate individuals to represent particular viewpoints about whether the plan should be built. Act out a council meeting where all the different views are discussed.

Most of the radioactivity is in the composition of the Earth's rocks and soil, a reminder of the great levels of radioactivity that existed when the Earth was formed millions of years ago. Without radioactivity there would be no sun and the Earth and all its inhabitants would never have been formed.

The main problem arises because we have discovered how to create radioactive substances for purposes such as medical diagnosis (X-rays) and harnessing nuclear power. Although it is a natural process, radioactivity can be very dangerous and has to be carefully controlled. Although nuclear power stations have a good safety record, there have been major incidents worldwide that have worried the public and drawn attention to the potential dangers of a nuclear disaster.

Alternative sources of energy **D**

Wind can turn windmills to create energy

Wave energy is produced by wind blowing over the sea

Solar energy comes from the sun

Tidal energy can be produced where fast flowing tides enter river estuaries (mouths)

Water, if it is fast flowing and continuous, produces hydro-electricity

Geothermal energy uses heat from inside the earth

With fossil fuels running out and the safety of nuclear power questioned, people are now looking at alternative forms of renewable energy, such as solar, wind and wave power.

The nuclear power industry receives millions of pounds a year for research. It is argued that this money could be directed towards conservation, greater energy efficiency and the use of renewable sources of energy. Protest groups point out that in this country 30% of electricity is produced by nuclear power, yet 30% of electricity produced is wasted. For every £1 spent on research into renewable energy, £80,000 has been spent on nuclear research. Although these figures are contested by the nuclear industry it is fair to conclude that governments, past and present, have not felt the need to prioritise research into 'renewables' and have not done enough to develop alternative energy sources.

In terms of sheer cost alone it would probably be more sensible to continue using nuclear energy, and we have to bear in mind the environmental price of exploiting any form of energy. People may think they are 'eco-friendly' but wind-farms and solar panels are noisy and visually intrusive and tidal power schemes can affect wildlife habitats.

The challenge is to ensure that nuclear power and the disposal of radioactive waste is, in the future, as safe as possible. The alternative must be to develop technologies that will harness renewable sources in an efficient and economical fashion to meet the world's energy needs in years to come.

E Wind farm

What do you think

Is nuclear power the great hope for the future of the planet or will it destroy us?

Old

Old: advanced in age or the later part of normal life.

Vintage cars, furniture and wines all increase in value as they age. Why not humans?

(BBC Lifeschool)

Hope I die before I get old.

(Pete Townshend, lead guitarist of The Who)

AIM

The unit examines how society's prejudices make many people fear growing old. Instead of regarding ageing as a natural development which occurs gradually over time, it tends to be seen as a time of loss and withdrawal from life.

We live in a society geared up to being young, beautiful and fit. Old age is embarrassing, a loss of influence and importance. Many people believe it is now time to look at the end of our life span and consider the rights of older people. For years political parties have been criticised for ignoring issues to do with ageing and old age. They appear to share a common belief that to be old is to be considered 'past it' or 'over the hill'.

Britain has an increasingly ageing population with over 10 million people of pensionable age, and the number of people aged over 85 is expected to double by the year 2015. Life expectancy has risen as medical technology, better diet and working conditions have improved. Survival into old age will now become normal, rather than the exception. How people feel about ageing depends on many factors. Some negative attitudes towards the older generation, often shown by young people, are in fact based on false impressions that must be challenged.

IN THE NEWS

AGEING: everyone's future!

You are as young as you feel

Needs of older people

Do we all want to be 100?

CHANGING STATUS – ELDERS OR OUTCASTS?

1 One of the headlines speaks of the 'needs' of elderly people. What do you think these are?

2 When you think about old people, what kind of ideas or images come into your head? Write down all these thoughts. Which can be described as positive and which as negative?

Compared with some cultures and societies, the developed countries tend to treat old people with very little respect. Despite changes in much of the Developing World, life goes on for older people as it always has. The extended family ensures that older relatives are valued and play an important role in family life. Traditionally no important decisions are made without first consulting the senior members of the community who still hold the most power and influence within their families. In many European countries the image of the elderly means that old people often feel left out, that there is little sense of caring for their worth. The traditional family structure has been eroded in many of these countries. Where once several generations would live in close proximity, now families are split up as individuals/couples have moved away to find work. Older people no longer play such an important role within their families and communities, and their influence has gradually weakened.

When asked how they feel about being 'old', many people respond by saying that though they may look old, they feel young inside. More elderly people are now able to lead more active and fulfilling lives than ever before, but for some growing old brings many unwanted problems.

THINK ABOUT

1 In pairs, discuss why a lot of people do not like the idea of growing old. What do you think they fear most?

2 Medical science may soon enable people to live much longer. Do you see this as a good thing?

3 What are the positive and negative aspects if we have an increasingly ageing population?

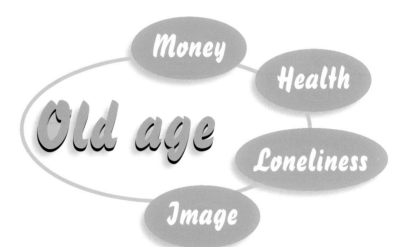

The main problems associated with old age

Money

Although some elderly people are well off, many experience a drop in income when they retire. State pensions in Britain are lower than most European countries and inevitably some find it very difficult to make ends meet.

Health

The older you get, the more likely you are to need health care. Recovery from broken bones and common illnesses such as colds and flu take far longer.

Loneliness

A lot of people have to face old age alone when their partners die. In Britain the changes in family structure mean that many are no longer close to their immediate relatives.

Image

Often, elderly people who have retired are no longer seen as contributing to society. The tremendous body of skills and knowledge that they have built up over the years are lost.

THE FIRST THING
SOME PEOPLE
NOTICE
IS HER AGE.

AGE *Concern*

LET'S MAKE AGE DISCRIMINATION A THING OF THE PAST.

B   Age Concern advertisement

THINK ABOUT

4 *In small groups try and think of some examples of television programmes where elderly people are portrayed as 'interfering' or 'miserable'. Are there any examples where older people are seen as individuals with positive characteristics?*

Activities

1   Many people often feel angry at the way they are portrayed in the media. In small groups, discuss the suggestion that older people should be 'seen and not blurred' by the media.

2   Discuss your ideas for creating a TV advert commissioned by the charity Help the Aged, whose main aim is to promote the image of the elderly.

3   Role-play or arrange an interview with an elderly person. Ask them about their life when they were young and how they feel now. What do they think about people's attitudes to the elderly? Discuss and note down the changes that have occurred in a person's life over many decades.

Many of the negative images about older people are promoted by the media. Too often, they are portrayed as frail and helpless, victims of poverty or crime or as figures of ridicule. The impression is given that all older people are vulnerable and weak. Television programmes and advertising in particular are often irresponsible in stereotyping older characters.

By stereotyping and ignoring the over-60s population, the media have been accused of reinforcing widespread gerontophobia (fear of ageing). Instead of emphasising negative images of dependency, illness and isolation, The Centre for Policy on Ageing believes that people should be described by four sociological stages (**C**).

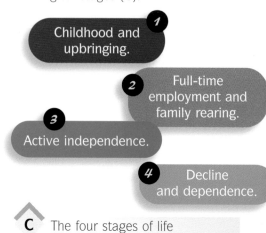

1   Childhood and upbringing.

2   Full-time employment and family rearing.

3   Active independence.

4   Decline and dependence.

C   The four stages of life

The 'Grey Panther' movement, which originated in America, fights for the cause of the elderly and is steadily increasing its strength in Britain. Companies are encouraged to have a policy of recruiting some older people. In this way age discrimination is stopped, more balanced workforces are created and there is less strain and reliance on pensions. Most importantly, the wealth of experience and knowledge built up over the years is not lost and can be passed on to the younger workforce.

Once you become aware of it ageism is apparent in many walks of life. Older people are rudely described as 'old fogies' or 'wrinklies' and they are frequently **patronised** in the way in which they are treated as children needing protection. Hospitals and doctors have been criticised for neglecting elderly patients whose need of treatment is regarded as too expensive for limited National Health budgets. The embarrassment so often expressed when older people continue to have an interest in sex or fashion is really a sad reflection on the rest of society.

The problem of ageism needs to be confronted as ruthlessly as does that of sexism and racism. It is important to remember that there is a strong likelihood that many of us will live to an old age. We should, therefore, have a vested interest in challenging ageist attitudes. If we do not we will, in turn, become victims of ageism.

D John Glenn – astronaut again at 77! (top)
Jack Nicklaus – golfing success in his late 50s (left)

What do you think

Why does an increasingly ageing population pose considerable problems for the future?

Poverty

Poverty: the state of being poor, struggling for even the basic necessities of life.

As long as there is poverty in the world I can never be rich, even if I have a million dollars.

(Martin Luther King, black civil rights leader)

The definition of poverty changes between countries, but the misery stays the same.

(Caroline Peer, Journalist)

AIM In this unit we examine the distinction between 'relative' and 'absolute' poverty and the efforts made to help with this worldwide problem.

Although the idea of poverty seems fairly straightforward, it is almost impossible to come up with an agreed standard of what poverty really is. Arguments about poverty can easily become bogged down in words. The reality of hardship facing millions of people today is easily lost.

When discussing poverty it is essential to understand what is meant from the start by the two terms: 'relative' and 'absolute'. In Britain there are families who, when compared with others, can be described as living in relative poverty. Being poor in this context is seen as having a standard of living below the normal acceptable level in any given society, going without 'luxuries'. It is important to remember that what were regarded as luxuries in one era – for example a fridge or central heating – can easily be seen as essentials of the next era.

When compared with the poorest in the Developing World, people living in relative poverty are regarded as quite well off. Millions of people in the Developing World live in absolute poverty. This means that they do not have sufficient money or food to supply their everyday basic needs. For example, lack of sufficient food to avoid starvation, of adequate shelter to avoid freezing, or of basic medicine to avoid preventable illness and disease.

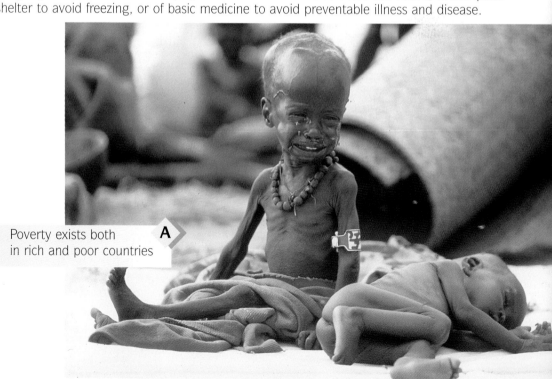

Poverty exists both in rich and poor countries **A**

Everyday needs in a wealthy developed country are not the same as those in a poor country so poverty does not have exactly the same meaning in different parts of the world.

In Britain today there are people living in relative poverty. For them not having a job or home or being poorly paid means they have great difficulty in changing their situation. The majority of people in the country survive comfortably, although admittedly some are much better off than others. In many countries however, every day is a struggle to survive for millions of people. They scrape a living from land which is totally inadequate and frequently devastated by civil war or natural disasters.

FIRE EXIT
KEEP
CLEAR

HOMELESS
AND
HUNGRY

IN THE NEWS

GAP BETWEEN RICH AND POOR WIDENS

World bank to focus on relief of poverty

EVERYDAY IS JUST SURVIVAL!

Families caught in the poverty trap

The pain of poverty

1 Which headlines do you think refer to the developing countries?

2 In your opinion, which headline sums up 'poverty'? Explain your choice.

3 Complete the following phrases with five responses.
a) To be rich means…
b) To be poor means…

Activities

1 Compare the two photographs (**A**). They show poverty in a developed and developing country. Discuss your reaction to the pictures. How do they show up the distribution of wealth throughout the world?

2 With a partner or in a group, imagine you are an individual in one of the situations shown in **A**. Explain how you came to be in your situation.

'Migrant Mother' – This photo, showing the suffering and poverty endured by people during the Great Depression in the US, shocked people worldwide

B

The Developed World – Relative poverty

A report in the early 1950s suggested that poverty in Britain had come close to disappearing because of the emerging **Welfare State**. During the **Great Depression** of the 1930s many people were living on the breadline and faced great difficulties. Most managed to survive on charity handouts and the support of relatives and friends. There was a general recognition that a rich country like the United States or Britain should be able to look after its poorest members (**B**).

Just after the Second World War, amid mounting concern about poverty, the Welfare State was created. Nowadays governments prefer to use the term 'below average income' rather than 'poverty'. Definitions of relative poverty focus on income levels said to be 'poor' in relation to the average or normal standards of living. However you define poverty, there are families who feel the serious effects of hardship and poverty and are in need of welfare benefits. Yet, despite these state benefits, food handouts and begging are still evident in most of the major cities throughout Britain. The effects of the suffering on particular individuals will vary but are likely to include some of the side-effects set out below:

- Living in a home that is cold or damp or not suitable for your needs.
- Not eating a healthy diet.
- Going hungry so your children do not.
- Suffering from poor health related to your living conditions and diet.
- Feelings of being alone and nobody caring.
- Living in run down areas with poor facilities.
- Feelings of being on the 'outside' of society and being helpless to do anything about it.
- Not bothering to vote because you believe nothing will change.
- Wearing clothes which are unsuitable or do not fit.
- Having no faith in the 'system'.
- Angry, frustrated and finally despairing.

C   Five minimum standards of living

One definition of poverty describes a set of five minimum standards, linked to a lack of adequate income, seen as basic requirements of 'citizenship'. If a person is deprived of these requirements in any way they are described as 'poor by exclusion' (**C**).

It is easy to point the finger of blame but in a developed country like Britain poverty is inexcusable. Most individuals and successive governments claim to be committed to getting rid of poverty but only actions will demonstrate this and ensure a future where all people can enjoy life, free from poverty.

Poverty by exclusion

1. **Adequate diet**
2. **Good health**
3. **Access to transport**
4. **Participation in community life**
5. **Opportunities to socialise**

Activities

3 Imagine what it would be like to struggle everyday because of poverty. Think carefully about your present lifestyle and make three lists to include:

a) The five activities you would most miss from your life now (like having a nice, hot bath or going out with friends).

b) The five luxuries you would have to go without (like the use of a phone or the television).

c) The five basic necessities you would miss most (like a clean bed or clothes).
Compare your list with others and discuss your choices.

4 How many items regarded as luxuries 20 years ago are now seen as essentials?

The Developing World – Absolute poverty

Wealth is not evenly distributed in the world and many developing countries are extremely poor. There are many reasons for this poverty (**D**).

Everybody has heard comments like, 'the trouble with these countries is overpopulation', or 'they should spend less money on weapons and more on food'. While important, it is clearly unrealistic to view these two factors as the root cause of poverty. Family planning programmes are making an impact. In 1965, the average couple in the developing world had just over six children. Today the number is slightly under four. In the 1980s, the numbers rose by 87 million each passing year – the highest ever. In the 1990s, that dropped to 81 million a year and population experts believe that if this can be sustained it should be possible to stabilise the world's population at around 8 billion in 2050. Previous estimates set the figure at around 12 or 13 billion.

What is undoubtedly true is that millions of people find themselves facing massive food shortages and are at the mercy of a combination of factors such as **war**, **natural disasters** and **economic collapse** often caused by massive debt problems.

NATURAL DISASTERS
INCREASING POPULATION
POLITICALLY UNSTABLE
Reasons for
POVERTY
UNABLE TO TRADE
DEBT REPAYMENT
INVOLVEMENT IN WARS

 **D** Absolute poverty

War

Too often poor countries are torn apart by civil war or hostilities with neighbouring countries. Many countries are politically unstable. Money which could be used to benefit the poor is directed into arms and military forces. People often become homeless within their own countries and become refugees.

Disasters

Natural disasters hit all parts of the world. When there was a serious drought in the mid-west of the United States in 1988, no one died. A similar disaster in some of the developing countries would have resulted in famine and starvation for millions. The difference lies in the storage of food and the ability to transport it as well as government aid to the farmers affected in the region. The developing countries face difficulties in organising effective rescue missions.

Debt

Many developing countries have borrowed money to finance developments but the loans have high interest charges. In a number of these countries, instead of increasing, the health and education budgets are extremely low. This is mainly because of the large allocation of resources for repaying foreign debt. Some world banks are now committed to writing off (cancelling) some of these debts to try and solve the situation.

THINK ABOUT

1   *'For years, overpopulation has been an excuse to explain poverty in the developing countries.' Is this a fair comment?*

2   *Why do the developed countries cope so much more easily with natural disasters than the developing ones?*

3   *Can you explain why enough food is produced to feed the world, yet every year millions face starvation?*

In 1980 an influential report was produced which examined the enormous problems of world poverty and put forward suggestions to resolve the issue. The 'North-South: A Programme for Survival' (known as the Brandt Report) referred to the divided world. The North or 'developed' world consisting of rich countries with a high standard of living (North America, Western Europe, Japan, Australia and New Zealand). The South or developing world consisting of poorer countries with a lower standard of living (most of Africa, Asia and South America). Whereas the North has a quarter of the world's population and four fifths of its income, the South has three quarters of the world's population and just one fifth of its income.

Activities

5   What was the Brandt Report and what were its main findings?

6   What is the message behind the cartoon in figure **E**?

7   Try to find out how one of the following organisations is helping to fight poverty in the developing world: United Nations, Oxfam, CARE, CAFOD, Action Aid, Christian Aid, Muslim Aid.

In its conclusion the Brandt Report made ten main suggestions:

- An end must be found to mass hunger and malnutrition. Money must be found to develop agriculture, irrigation, crop storage, fertilisers and other aids.

- Ensure that money goes into direct help rather than weapon production.

- Increase overseas aid.

- Developing countries should increase their earnings by having more say in the processing, marketing and distribution of their exported goods.

- More attention should be paid to educating the public about the need for international cooperation.

- An emergency programme is essential to help the world's poorest nations particularly in the poverty belts of Asia and Africa.

- Greater international support for family planning programmes.

- An international 'income tax' to spread wealth more evenly.

- The international monetary system must be changed to give the developing countries a greater advantage.

- A World Development Fund could be developed to distribute the resources raised on a universal and automatic basis.

Poverty remains a global issue and people are beginning to understand that whatever happens in one part of the world will affect another. Millions of people in the South are starving and disease-ridden. It is easy to blame this situation on population growth and general lack of development. This view is just too simplistic. It is hypocritical to complain about overpopulation in the South, while ignoring overconsumption in the North. More developed societies have a responsibility to change their lifestyles and their consumption patterns and to make better use of their technology. There needs to be dialogue between the North and the less developed South. A commitment to share the world's resources more equally is the only way to fight the global issue of poverty.

E   The cartoonist's view – 'We're all in the same boat'

F Grain mountain

What do you think ❓

Frank Buchman once said: 'There is enough in the world for everyone's need, but not enough for everyone's greed'. Can you see any changes happening to this problem in your lifetime?

Quality

donorcard

AIM

Quality: 'the degree of excellence of a thing' or 'a system of maintaining standards'.

> *Life's not just about being alive, but being well.*
> (Marcus Valerius Martial, Latin poet, AD c40–104)

> *Though medicine may succeed in dramatically extending life, at times it does so without having secured a quality of life which is acceptable to those whose lives are prolonged.*
> (David Smith, Author)

The unit examines some of the developments in medical technology and questions whether there are any limits to the search for 'quality of life'.

Medical advances sometimes make it difficult for doctors to decide what action is in the best interests of their patients. Sometimes the decision may be fairly straightforward, but in life and death decisions such as euthanasia and abortion we often hear the term 'expected quality of life'. Today, the guiding principle for doctors seems to be to value human life and improve its quality if possible.

Developments in medical technology over the past four decades have re-focused the debate on the quality of life. Through the use of transplants, assisted reproduction and cosmetic surgery the lives of hundreds of thousands of people have been transformed. Developments in genetic engineering also offer hope for those suffering from genetic illnesses.

Opinions are divided over whether these developments are beneficial. Some people describe them as 'frivolous' or 'interfering with nature'. Supporters, on the other hand, claim that medical ethics should be concerned with the physical and mental health of an individual, not just the ability to keep the body organs functioning.

IN THE NEWS

Quality of life – but at what expense?

Human use of animal organs will become routine

HOPE FOR CHILDLESS COUPLES

Why don't we let nature take its course?

Born or made?

1 What do you think is meant by the headline 'Quality of life – but at what expense?'

2 Should we allow nature to 'take its course'?

THINK ABOUT

1 *In your opinion, should medicine be looking to preserve life or improve life?*

2 *In pairs, look through the bulleted list below and decide what your priorities would be if you were in charge of resources for a hospital. Bear in mind four views often put forward about medicine:*
   a) *research is vital;*
   b) *saving life must be the top priority;*
   c) *prevention is better than cure;*
   d) *the disadvantaged must be given priority.*

   ● *Funding a unit researching 'test-tube' baby techniques.*
   ● *Supporting AIDS research.*
   ● *Improving breast cancer screening programmes.*
   ● *Developing plastic surgery techniques.*
   ● *Setting up healthy eating and diet programmes in local clinics.*
   ● *Funding research into organ transplantation.*

Organ transplants

Since the first successful kidney transplant in 1950, people have been able to lead fuller lives. In 1994 an Englishman's life was saved because he had six organs transplanted into his body. Every year over 7,000 people in Britain suffer kidney failure and about one third of these die because of the lack of any available treatment. A question is often raised concerning transplants from dead **donors** in order to increase the supply. At the present time, a person has to 'opt in' to allow an organ transplantation after death. Consent comes with the carrying of a donor card or permission from the next of kin being obtained. Some medical authorities would like the law changed so that rather than opting in, an individual would have to 'opt out' by refusing to allow organs to be removed after death.

In the past, the failure of a major organ normally meant death or incapacitation. Now, thanks to very successful methods of treatment this need not be the case. Kidney, heart, liver and cornea transplants are now commonplace and effective operations. The youngest person to receive a liver transplant was just five days old. The baby girl had collapsed just 24 hours after she was born and an immediate transplant was necessary to save her life. Without the donation of a liver from a dead 10 year-old child she would have died within two weeks. As her father said: 'a tragedy in somebody's life may bring someone else happiness'.

There are still concerns, however, with the use of certain body parts such as the brain, or use of xenotransplants (organs from animals). Also in countries where human rights are open to abuse, people can be exploited. It is a well known fact that the body can survive with just one kidney and so some people choose to sell one, raising money to help their family.

A A donor card

Activities

1 What are the advantages of a donor card?

2 Do you think organs should be used automatically, unless the person has specifically requested otherwise?

Assisted reproduction

In vitro fertilisation (IVF) has given hope to thousands of couples who encounter difficulties in having children. Until the scientific breakthrough of IVF in 1978 these couples would have either had to go through adoption procedures or accept that they could not have children.

Infertility can sometimes badly affect a relationship, putting a couple under a great deal of strain. Fertility drugs and the use of IVF techniques which can include sperm injection, donor eggs and frozen embryos are now available. Which of the procedures a specialist will use depends largely on the reason a couple are encountering difficulties (**B**).

Advances in assisted reproduction

Fertility drugs	These cause more than one egg to be produced each month.	Donor egg	Eggs are taken from a donor and after IVF treatment are then implanted into another woman.
In vitro fertilisation	Eggs are taken from the woman's ovaries and placed in a glass petri dish. After fertilisation the embryos begin to develop and are then placed in the uterus.	Frozen eggs	A woman's eggs can be collected and frozen for thawing and fertilisation at a later date.
Sperm injection	Using an ultrafine needle a single sperm is injected into the egg to fertilise it.	Frozen embryo	Extra embryos created during the IVF process can be frozen and stored for future use.

B

The development of these reproductive technologies has also transformed the practice of surrogacy ('womb leasing'). Historically, couples who were unable to have children could sometimes ask a female relative/friend to be the biological mother of their child. Now, because of the advances in medical technology, there are different types of surrogacy:

- Artificial insemination (AI) surrogacy. An embryo is created with the sperm of the intended father and egg of the surrogate who will carry the baby.

- IVF surrogacy. An embryo is created by the intended parents and then transferred to the surrogate.

- Donor surrogacy. An embryo is created by using either the sperm of the intended father to fertilise a donor egg or the egg of the intended mother is fertilised by donor sperm and then carried by the surrogate. In some cases neither of the intended parents are actually a biological parent.

Numerous concerns have been expressed over these techniques particularly when the intended parents are not the biological parents and when the surrogate is paid for her services.

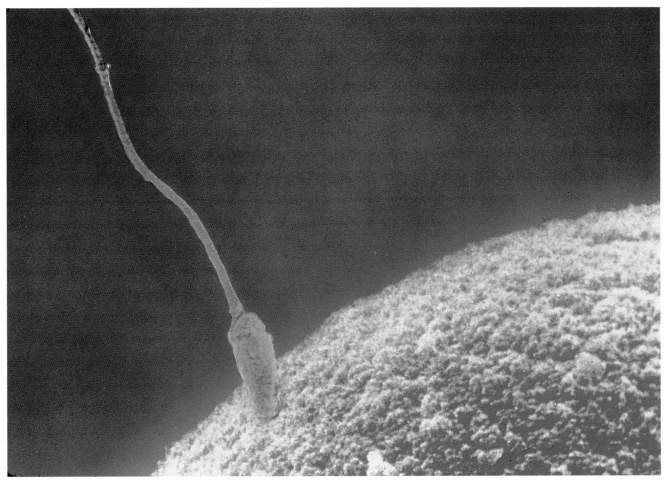

C The moment of conception

IVF, fertility drugs and other techniques have revolutionised conception. Today, scientists are pushing the technology of assisted reproduction even further. One such medical procedure is 'sex selection' giving hope to thousands of couples who are at risk of passing on serious diseases such as haemophilia (which only affects the male) to their children. IVF technology means that male and female embryos can be identified at a very early stage of development. In the case of haemophilia, it is possible to ensure that women at risk will conceive only girls and thereby increase their chances of having healthy children.

Medicines and high-tec procedures have utterly transformed the treatment of infertility and without doubt have significantly improved the quality of many people's lives. At the same time, however, we must realise that some of the medical techniques for assisting conceptions continue to cause a lot of controversy.

Activities

3 What dangers could arise if sex selection was openly available to couples?

4 In your opinion, do the advantages of sex selection outweigh the disadvantages?

5 The fertility methods described in **B** are considered to be perfectly acceptable by many people. What do you think about these methods?

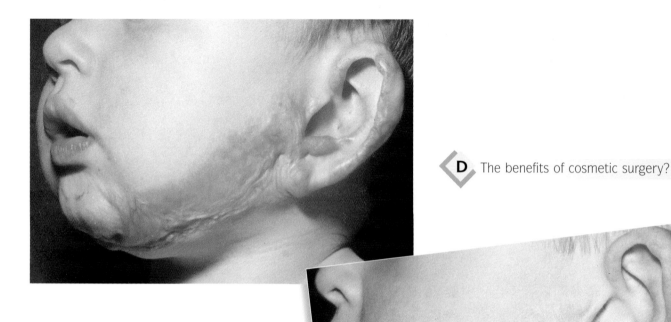

D   The benefits of cosmetic surgery?

Cosmetic surgery

The earliest recorded cosmetic operation took place in Italy during the sixteenth century. A surgeon attempted to reconstruct a man's nose damaged in a fight, from bits of his upper arm. Cosmetic surgery grew more acceptable and widespread after the First World War as reconstructive surgery was needed for injured soldiers. The operations were clearly not for vanity but rather to help people, both psychologically and socially, to overcome horrific injuries.

Every year in the United States, over 2.5 million people undergo cosmetic surgery and it is now regarded as very much part of everyday life. It is also becoming increasingly acceptable here in Britain. In the past few years, however, many aspects of this surgery have received bad publicity in the media. Barely a decade ago there were only a few 'aesthetic' cosmetic surgeons operating in Britain. Today, there are hundreds and every year the number of people requesting surgery increases. Many of the requests come from middle-aged people anxious to avoid the ageing process. Others say looking good gives them confidence. Yet, for thousands of people who are disfigured as the result of accidents or have birth defects the psychological and social benefits of these operations cannot be overstated.

THINK ABOUT

3   In small groups discuss the following:

   a) What are the benefits of cosmetic surgery?

   b) Is cosmetic surgery about self respect or glamour?

'When the time comes, I am going to have a face-lift, jaw-lift, eye-lift. Everything that's falling will be lifted. And the things that can't be lifted will be moved.'

   c) Is saying that they are unhappy with the way they look a sufficiently good reason for a person to request an operation?

Plastic surgery techniques designed for accident patients are increasingly sophisticated and recovery from operation is now much easier and faster. Already the use of laboratory-grown skin is widespread for burn victims, and the idea of 'spare parts' surgery is no longer the stuff of science fiction. **Lasers** are used for resurfacing the face and to cut with great accuracy, and **keyhole surgery** leaves smaller scars. Both techniques enable surgeons to carry out previously radical operations with the minimum amount of bleeding and bruising. Research is now also looking at ways of speeding up wound healing so procedures will be faster and healing could happen a day after an operation.

The problem still remains that some people request treatment they do not really need, seeking cosmetic surgery simply because they are not happy with the way they look. Others, however, seem to be far more deserving. Through no fault of their own, people can be badly disfigured and most people agree that if modern medical technology can help then it should be available.

CASE STUDIES

Choose one of the following case studies and decide where the priorities lie and whether you feel cosmetic surgery is justified.

A

A teenager is anxious about a birthmark on their face. Although the mark is small and barely seen the individual is becoming reluctant to go to school and go out with friends.

B

A middle-aged man involved in a car crash is badly burnt on his arms. A series of skin grafts would help him recover, but the operations will be performed over a long period of time and some scarring will be permanent.

C

A young woman has requested a breast enlargement. She is increasingly anxious about her appearance and insists that her relationships are badly affected by her concerns.

Activity

6 In groups of three, choose one of the case studies opposite and role-play an interview between the doctor and the concerned individual. The third member of your group can act as an observer, noting down the key points being made. Take it in turns to play the different roles.

It is clear that the quality of life for an individual can be greatly increased by modern medical techniques such as organ transplants. Some people will argue that if a person's quality of life improves even from some minor cosmetic surgery then it is worthwhile. It is suggested by some, that in an overpopulated world, childless couples should just accept their problem of infertility. Others point out that a couple's quality of life can be transformed by having a child. The problems clearly arise when the boundaries between good and dubious practice are increasingly blurred. Unfortunately, the interpretation of the word 'quality' means different things to different people.

What do you think

'Some believe that certain medical developments are being used for trivial reasons rather than improving the quality of life.'

Do we now regard human life as a product to be ordered rather than as a gift?

Racism

Racism: prejudice or discrimination which is determined by the belief that one race is superior to others.

Racism robs people of their humanity. Racism is a denial of human dignity.

(The Humanist Manifesto)

If you live in a world where everything positive is white, and you are black, then you soon become disillusioned.

(Angella Johnson – BBC Lifeschool)

AIM This unit looks at some of the issues underlying racism, in particular the way in which racial hatred is caused by fear, fuelled by ignorance.

Throughout history people have been persecuted for many reasons, such as religion, sex, social class, age or nationality. While some of these forms of **persecution** have largely been eliminated from our society, others still remain. Because of the colour of their skin or country of origin, millions of people are deprived of the fair treatment that most of us take for granted. Unfortunately, racism still exists today and it is the root cause of tremendous suffering for millions of people.

The conquests of Africa, America and Asia led to the destruction of cultures and civilisations. Racism was used to justify the slave trade which led to the forced removal of millions of people from Africa. Anyone who was not a white European was regarded as less human and treated accordingly. Before Europeans had discovered these lands other races had been actively involved in slavery.

With conquest came exploitation of the lands. Throughout the eighteenth and nineteenth centuries Britain used its colonies, destroying the local trade and commerce, replacing them with produce for its own needs such as tea, timber and rubber. The result of this was that many colonies were totally dependent on the colonial power or so-called 'mother country', and consequently had agricultural systems which could not support their own populations.

Even throughout the twentieth century certain individuals have tried to prove that some races were inferior, claiming that they had smaller brains and were less intelligent. The science of genetics has showed these ideas to be ridiculous. A human being's physical make up depends on approximately 100,000 genes and well over 90% of these are similar in everyone.

The problem of racism lies in attitude, in the fear and ignorance people have of others who do not look the same as they do.

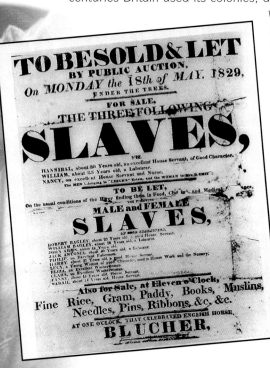

TO BE SOLD & LET

BY PUBLIC AUCTION.

On MONDAY the 18th of MAY, 1829,

UNDER THE TREES.

FOR SALE,

THE THREE FOLLOWING

SLAVES,

VIZ.

HANNIBAL, about 30 Years old, an excellent House Servant, of Good Character.

WILLIAM, about 35 Years old, a Labourer.

NANCY, an excellent House Servant and Nurse.

The MEN belonging to "LEECH'S" Estate, and the WOMAN to Mrs. D. SMIT

TO BE LET,

On the usual conditions of the Hirer finding them in Food, Clothes, and Medical

THE FOLLOWING

MALE and FEMALE

SLAVES,

OF GOOD CHARACTERS.

ROBERT BAGLEY, about 20 Years old, a good House Servant.

WILLIAM BAGLEY, about 18 Years old, a Labourer.

JOHN ALMA, about 13 Years old.

JACK ANTONIA, about 40 Years old, a Labourer.

PHILIP, an Excellent Fisherman.

HARRY, about 27 Years old, a good House Servant.

LUCY, a Young Woman of good Character, used in House Work and the Nursery.

ELIZA, an Excellent Washerwoman.

CLARA, an Excellent Washerwoman.

FANNY, about 14 Years old, House Servant.

SARAH, about 11 Years old, House Servant.

Also for Sale, at Eleven o'Clock,

Fine Rice, Gram, Paddy, Books, Muslins,

Needles, Pins, Ribbons, &c. &c.

AT ONE O'CLOCK, THAT CELEBRATED ENGLISH HORSE,

BLUCHER,

 A The slave trade

IN THE NEWS

JUDGE CONDEMNS RACIST GROUP AS VILE AND EVIL

When racism wins, the sport loses

GUARDSMAN WAS VICTIM OF RACE BIAS

Harassed Asians 'fatalistic' over attacks

Not just a question of black and white

1 Why do you think some people grow up to be racially prejudiced?

2 What are the 'messages' behind the headlines, , 'Harassed Asians "fatalistic" over attacks' and 'When racism wins, the sport loses'?

One of the main problems in examining racism is that the terms people use may mean different things at different times, even though people believe they are talking about the same thing. Racism is brought about by prejudice, discrimination, and stereotyping. These three terms are central but not unique to the racism debate. All can be applied to aspects such as sex, social class or age. Even left-handed people can feel discriminated against as many objects are designed for right-handed users.

PREJUDICE – an attitude of mind where someone prejudges others from a different racial group. It is a way of thinking about others which will not change even in the light of new experience.

DISCRIMINATION – basically prejudice in action. Discrimination occurs when a person is unfairly treated because of their differences to the people who are discriminating.

STEREOTYPING – creating a fixed image (stereotype) in three different stages:

a) take some easily identified features that a group supposedly has;
b) make these features the dominant characteristics of the group;
c) suggest that all members of the group possess these features.

These 'stereotypes' are then used as a basis for racial abuse and help reinforce prejudices.

RACISM – the superiority of one race above all others. Racism occurs when racial prejudice is turned into action of some sort, and this action harms another group of people.

B The racism route

Activities

1 In pairs or groups think of an example of how prejudice can turn into discrimination. Appoint someone to act as a spokesperson and report your views to the rest of the class.

2 Over a period of a few days note down any racist incidents you see on television or read in newspapers and try to find news items or stories which are concerned with one or more of the 'routes of racism'. Which reports are about explicit racism, and which show more subtle prejudices?

RACISM

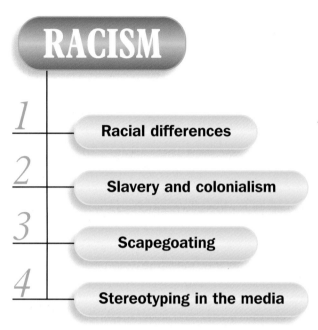

1 **Racial differences**

2 **Slavery and colonialism**

3 **Scapegoating**

4 **Stereotyping in the media**

When looking at the racism that black people in particular have experienced and continue to experience in this country, the causes appear to come from four main sources (**C**).

C Causes of racism

Racial differences

In the eighteenth century the view was established that there are certain unchangeable and basic differences between races. The Swedish botanist, Carolus Linnaeus, classified humans into three distinct races based on physical differences – Negroid, Caucasian and Mongoloid. Some writers used his work to conclude that the Caucasian race was 'superior' because of the dominating culture of Western Europe at that time.

Slavery and colonialism

In the eighteenth century Britain had more colonies than any other empire in the history of the world, and was largely responsible for the transportation of millions of West Africans to be used as slaves. One of the arguments in favour of slavery was that it helped to civilise 'inferior' black people by bringing them into contact with the 'superior' white culture.

Nazi propaganda　**D**

Activity

3 This poster (**E**) was designed to celebrate the European Year Against Racism.
   a) What message is the image giving you?
   b) Who is the poster aimed at?
   c) What is the poster saying about racists?

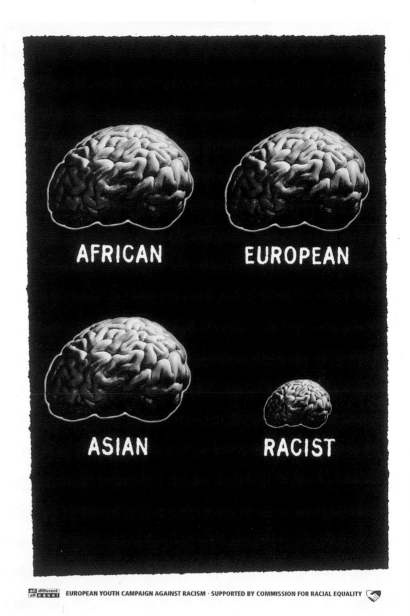

AFRICAN   EUROPEAN

ASIAN   RACIST

EUROPEAN YOUTH CAMPAIGN AGAINST RACISM · SUPPORTED BY COMMISSION FOR RACIAL EQUALITY

E

Scapegoating

The term scapegoat has biblical origins in an annual ritual where a goat, representing all the sins of everyone in a community, was driven out into the wilderness and everyone felt better. In other words, scapegoating is finding someone to blame. During the 1930s the Nazi Party made frequent use of scapegoats and stereotypes in their propaganda (**D**). They succeeded in convincing some people that the Jews were responsible for Germany's unemployment and economic problems. The Nazis pursued their racism to the extreme conclusion – the Holocaust.

Stereotyping and the media

In the past the media has reinforced stereotyped attitudes and promoted the idea that some ethnic groups can be a problem. During the 1980s the tabloid press was criticised for suggesting that young black people were more criminally inclined than young whites. During the 1990s a real effort has been made by the media to avoid reinforcing prejudices, offering a more balanced and responsible portrayal of ethnic groups. The fact that 1997 was declared the European Year Against Racism offers hope that attitudes are changing.

In the past, the Law Courts have been accused of not taking vicious and dangerous racial abuse seriously enough. The 1976 Race Relations Act strengthened the two previous laws of 1965 and 1968. Now every person is legally protected against racial discrimination in employment, housing, education, and the provision of goods and services. The Act also outlawed 'incitement to racial hatred'. Prosecutions, however, are still relatively rare and despite the efforts of many organisations and the authorities, racism is still apparent in Britain today.

In Britain the law has had to act against extreme right-wing political groups – 'neo-nazis' – who regard Hitler as a hero and publish material intended to stir up racial hatred. The threatening, abusive and insulting material is directed against racial, ethnic and religious minorities and their supporters, and also targets individuals. One such publication gave precise details on how to make lethal car bombs and ammonia filled **Molotov cocktails** designed to burn holes in a victim's lungs.

THINK ABOUT

1 *In small groups examine the reasons why it might be difficult to make the Race Relations Act work. Discuss whether you think the Act has been worth having.*

2 *How much racism do you see today? Does it depend on where you live? Is our society more or less racist than it used to be?*

F Race and sport: Tommie Smith and John Carlos (left); Jesse Owens (above right)

THERE ARE LOTS OF PLACES IN BRITAIN WHERE RACISM DOESN'T EXIST.

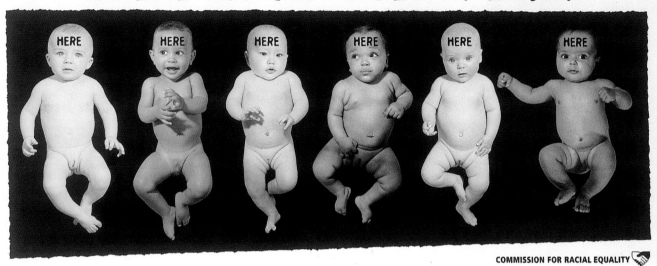

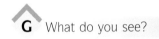

COMMISSION FOR RACIAL EQUALITY

G   What do you see?

Incidents at sports events throughout the world have frequently highlighted the continued problem of racism. Three of the most famous occasions were witnessed in the 1936, 1968 and 1972 Olympic games. In the 1936 games in Berlin, the black American athlete Jesse Owens won four gold medals and rubbished the Nazis' racist ideology. Thirty two years later, Tommie Smith and John Carlos won medals for coming first and third in the 200m. As the American national anthem played, both men gave a clenched fist black power salute (**F**). It was their protest against racism in America; as a result both men were condemned by the sport and by their country. The 1972 Munich games witnessed a further example of the hostilities that have long existed between the Arabs and the Jews. Arab terrorists infiltrated the area where 10,000 athletes were staying and killed 11 Israeli Olympians.

Even today black sporting success often disguises the fact that it has been achieved in spite of racist attitudes. Incredibly, some racists at football matches abuse and insult opposition players while at the same time applauding the efforts of their own players, black or white! Sport mirrors the rest of society in that ethnic minorities are still concentrated in less powerful roles. The vast majority are the performers, very few hold the managerial or administrative posts. Sports authorities are now acting far more quickly and with greater determination to stamp out racist attitudes, but it still exists.

What do you think ?

Is racism still a problem in Britain today? What more do you think we could do to rid society of racism?

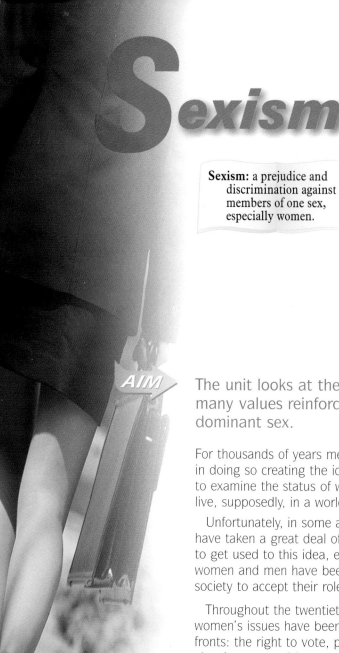

Sexism

Sexism: a prejudice and discrimination against members of one sex, especially women.

Whatever women do they must do twice as well as men to be thought half as good.

(Charlotte Whitton)

If it were a lady, it would get its bottom pinched.

(Fiat advert)

If this lady was a car she would run you down.

(Anon)

AIM The unit looks at the way that society is run and the way in which its many values reinforce the belief that men see themselves as the dominant sex.

For thousands of years men have dominated societies, controlling the wealth and power and in doing so creating the ideas which have left women as second-class citizens. It is difficult to examine the status of women during this time because generally they had none. We now live, supposedly, in a world where women are treated equally and with respect.

Unfortunately, in some areas it seems to have taken a great deal of time and effort to get used to this idea, especially where women and men have been conditioned by society to accept their roles.

Throughout the twentieth century, women's issues have been fought on several fronts: the right to vote, pro-choice abortion, rape crisis centres, fair settlement in divorce cases and equality in the workplace and in society, to name a few. With each new generation comes fresh hope that eventually the barriers will disappear and women and men will be equal.

The barriers, however, often remain in place and sexism can be seen in the ways in which women are treated and often exploited for the benefit of men. Our language is often sexist and our advertising continues to exploit women. Pornography almost always targets men and is one of the biggest growth industries in the world. Over half of Britain's population is female yet this is not truly reflected in government. Despite fairly recent moves in the Church of England, most Christian denominations do not allow women to hold any positions of power.

SHE. IT IS TIME I GOT OUT OF THIS PLACE. WHERE SHALL I FIND THE KEY?

CONVICTS
LUNATICS
AND
WOMEN!
HAVE NO VOTE
FOR PARLIAMENT

 Protest poster!

IN THE NEWS

Boys are the weaker sex in exams

The hand that rocks the cradle rules the world

MEN CONVINCED THAT WOMEN ARE LESS INTELLIGENT

Behind every man there's a low-paid woman

Women still lag behind in pay and job stakes

1 Examine the five headlines.
   a) What do you think are the meanings behind the headlines, 'Behind every man there's a low-paid woman' and 'The hand that rocks the cradle rules the world'?
   b) Why do women still lag behind men in the pay and job stakes?
   c) Why do you think there are still more men than women in high paid jobs?

Generally there are more women in work than ever before but our workplaces remain sexist – women have the lesser paid jobs and poorer pensions, are subjected to sexual harassment and are less likely to attain the top positions in industry and commerce. Although women's entry into professions such as medicine or law, for example, is now on a par with that of men, they still account for few senior members. Women are still often denied access to promotion, either by the prejudice of employers, or the lack of child care facilities meaning they have to sacrifice their career if they want to start a family.

Sexism in society   **B**

THINK ABOUT

1 Discuss which of the eight areas in **B** is the most damaging for women's rights. Give reasons for your answer.

2 Can you think of any other areas in society where women are openly discriminated against?

3 In groups, discuss what you think of women who model topless or naked. Are they allowing themselves to be exploited, or are they exploiting men?

4 What influence do you think pornographic magazines and films have in forming men's attitudes towards women? Does pornography encourage violence against women?

Controversial sexist images?

Activities

1   Can you think of examples of adverts where women on the one hand are stereotyped as the mother or carer and on the other hand are presented as the equals/superiors of men?

List them in a table like the one below:

Mother/carer	Equal/superior

2   In households, which tasks are nearly always done by women? Have things changed in recent years? If so, in what ways? What are the reasons why some household jobs are nearly always done by men and others by women?

3   'Bring this letter, and your wife, with you.' (Letter from HM Inspector of Taxes.)

Explain why this statement is blatantly sexist.

For a long time sexism has been a talking point in the advertising world but in the last few years we have seen an interesting development. For years there have been numerous complaints about women being used in a sexist way to advertise anything from cars to mineral water. These advertisements always tend to show a certain type of woman, who is young and often adopting a provocative position. In most advertising there is little mention of the kind of 'new man' who is as likely as their female partner to be doing the washing up.

Towards the end of the 1990s however, the portrayal of women in advertising began to reflect the reality of women's lives. The advertising industry worked hard to get away from the depiction of the traditional 'washing-up and cleaning' role for women. Almost immediately the Advertising Standards Authority started to receive complaints from the public about posters described as offensive, sexist, sadistic and promoting images of violence against men.

One campaign by a jeans manufacturer showed a woman's stiletto-heeled boot pushing down on the buttocks of a naked man under the words, 'Put the boot in'. The manufacturers insisted that their advert was not indecent because it was light-hearted and reflected the changes in society towards women.

Despite a supposed revolution in relationships, men are often still absent from the domestic front. A study of working parents disclosed that, while women frequently think of their children or domestic responsibilities while at work, men rarely, if ever, do. Even today, from an early age the majority of young children take a narrow view of sex roles around the family home. The women are still depicted washing-up, cooking, cleaning, and caring for the children whereas the men are repairing cars, decorating, gardening and going out to work.

Even at school opportunities for boys and girls can be restricted because of these attitudes. The majority of senior teaching posts are held by men, certain GCSE subjects are seen as mainly the choice of one particular sex, and career ambitions have long been solely directed at boys.

'Meanwhile, back in the Fifties…
The Good Wife's Guide'

- Have dinner ready. Plan ahead to have a delicious meal ready, on time for his return.

- Clear away the clutter.

- Greet him with a warm smile and show sincerity in your desire to please him.

- Listen to him. Let him talk first – remember, his topics of conversation are more important than yours.

- Your goal: Try to make sure your home is a place of peace, order and tranquillity where your husband can renew himself in body and spirit.

- Don't ask him questions about his actions or question his judgement or integrity. Remember he is the master of the house. You have no right to question him.

- A good wife always knows her place.

Traditionally the woman has been expected to undertake the role of wife, mother and carer. This work has largely been undervalued and unrewarded. Over the last 20 years, however, the role of women in society has undergone a drastic review. It is now more widely accepted that women need spend no more time than men in looking after the family and home and, if they wish, they should be able to pursue a rewarding career path of their own. Today many are income earners and the rights of women are increasingly on the public agenda.

Clearly some of the roles of the sexes have changed and continue to evolve in most societies. It is probably fair to say that there is now a far greater degree of equality in men and women's relationships and in many areas of society than there has ever been. Attitudes towards recognising the proper role of women in society are beginning to change. That said, there is still a long way to go before true equality is achieved.

Activity

4 Read through 'Meanwhile, back in the Fifties… The Good Wife's Guide'. In pairs act out a scene in which one person, who holds sexist views and agrees with the 'guide', is being persuaded by a second person that times have changed! Compare your arguments and thoughts with other pairs or groups.

What do you think

Why is the situation between men and women so unbalanced in today's world?

Taboo

Taboo: a prohibition or restriction imposed by social custom. Something which is to be avoided or not discussed.

Why fear death? It is the most beautiful adventure in life.

(Charles Frohman)

Death is nature's way of telling you to slow down.

(Life Insurance proverb)

AIM The unit examines why death evokes so many powerful feelings and emotions and why, to many people, it is the ultimate taboo.

Television programmes show numerous scenes of death, ranging from the horrific to the peaceful, and some are even ridiculous. News reports often present death in the same way as a sports bulletin or weather forecast. Television makes it easy to forget that death is very real and involves grief and pain for those people involved. To say that death in our society is taboo is an understatement. The fear of death is understandable because it is the fear of the unknown. Death is the one certainty of life. We focus on controlling life. People live longer, stay fitter but death remains out of our control.

THINK ABOUT

1 *Look at the explanations given below for why people feel awkward talking about death. Are any of them good reasons? Explain why.*

- *Other people find it embarassing.*
- *Most of us are so afraid of death we prefer not to talk about it.*
- *People might think you are* morbid *if you talk about death and dying.*
- *We tend to focus on life rather than think about death.*

2 *Below are some of the reasons why people believe it is important to talk about death. Do you agree or disagree with them?*

- *It is only by talking things through that people can overcome their fears.*
- *Everyone knows their friends and relatives will die one day and so it is important to think about it.*
- *If we talk about death we may find out that other people also share our worries and concerns.*
- *Talking about death means an individual's wishes can be properly met after their death.*

IN THE NEWS

Talking about death – the great taboo

Nobody lives forever!

DEATH – THE INOPERABLE DISEASE

1 When you think of the word death, what thoughts and feelings come into your mind?

Why we must not fear death

FOREVER YOUNG

2 What reasons do people give for being afraid of death? Which of these apply to you?

A hundred years ago in Britain most families would have had real experience of death. Standards of living and medicine have gradually changed our view of death. Before the two World Wars, people were unafraid to share their grief with one another. The coffin containing the dead person remained in the house until the day of the funeral so relatives and friends could pay their 'last respects'. Death was regarded as a natural part of the order of things. The death of millions in the two World Wars changed this attitude. Death became more remote. Hundreds of thousands of bodies were never returned home as they were buried abroad in war cemeteries, other bodies were never even found.

Today we attempt to hide death. In Britain alone over 700,000 people die every year. Roughly three quarters of these deaths take place in hospitals or hospices, 'out of sight, out of mind'. Far fewer people die at home but when they do a professional undertaker will usually remove the body as quickly as possible.

In the developing countries death is almost part of everyday routine. The pain of losing someone is still there, but parents almost expect to lose several of their children within a few years of their birth. They learn to cope with their grief far better than their counterparts in the more developed countries.

Loss is part of the human condition, but coming to terms with the death of a loved one can be extremely traumatic. Each year over 10,000 young people lose a parent. Many experts now believe that young people in particular are sheltered from death far too much. Often the 'English stiff upper lip' is blamed because unlike other countries and cultures we do not encourage outward signs of emotion. Despite being sympathetic, most people are very awkward in the company of someone who has been recently bereaved.

A War – a time to live, a time to die

CLARENCE E. JACOBUS
PVT HI M G BATT N 29 DIV
NEW JERSEY OCT 24 1918

THINK ABOUT

3 Do you think it is better to shelter young people from death?

4 Should we return to former times when people died in the family home surrounded by relatives and friends?

5 If a relative is dying should a child be told no matter what their age?

In contrast, in Mexico every year there is the celebration of the Day of the Dead. To Mexicans, this is a positive way of dealing with the loss of people they love. It is an outward sign that the dead have not been forgotten and are still loved. This clearly helps to unite people, especially children who find the idea of death much easier to cope with. To many Westerners, who prefer to avoid the subject altogether, this is seen as a rather morbid practice.

Stages in grief

Shock

For a period of time after the death there is a great deal of sadness.

Denial

It is not uncommon for some people to refuse to accept that a loved one has died.

Anger

The grieving person asks: 'Why did they have to die? Why them?'

Guilt

Arguments are often remembered and some blame themselves for not having had better relationships in the past.

Adjustment

Depending on the character and strength of the bereaved, life begins to go back to 'normal'.

B Day of the Dead festival in Mexico, 2 November

In understanding how people cope with the loss of someone close to them it is important to recognise that there are several stages that people go through. All these feelings are quite common and normal (**C**).

Everyone goes through a process of mourning but obviously some people deal with the trauma of death better than others. Much depends on the love and support of relatives and close friends.

Attitudes to death are often bound up with particular faiths. Though not required by law, most people feel the need for some kind of religious ceremony after a person has died. Most Christians have no problem with burial or the **cremation** of a dead body. In the past, Christians believed that a life lived according to God's rules would be rewarded with a place in heaven, whereas a life which ignored God's rules would result in punishment in hell. Nowadays, some Christians find it difficult to accept the idea of a God punishing people by sending them to hell. The funeral service within the Christian tradition expresses a clear belief that death is not the end, but a gateway to a new life.

Burials in the Jewish faith are usually very basic as a reminder that people are born in the world equal, and should leave it the same way. A Jewish burial is followed by a week of mourning called the 'Shiva'. During this time friends bring food to the grieving relatives so that they do not have to worry about things like everyday chores. Hindus and Sikhs always cremate dead bodies whereas Jews and Muslims always bury them.

Activity

1 Imagine that a parent of a close friend has just died. What sort of things would you wish to tell your friend?

D A Muslim funeral

The Muslim scriptures clearly state that the body must be buried, believing that it will be raised to life again on the Day of Judgement. Death is not a taboo word for Muslims as after death there is the promise of everlasting life. During a Muslim funeral many people get involved and this without doubt helps with the grieving process. Hindus believe in **reincarnation**. The soul (Atman) is immortal and is continually reborn. Death is not the end but merely the separation of the soul from the body. Cremation allows the soul to be released and proceed to it's next life. Most of the world's major faiths believe in some form of life after death and this is usually connected with how people have lived on earth and whether they have followed their faith.

Some people become incredibly insecure when facing death. Certain individuals are so obsessed with avoiding death that they will go to any lengths to extend their life. In the United States people, have paid to have their bodies (or at least their heads) preserved indefinitely in liquid nitrogen. This technique is known as cryonics. The hope is to freeze a patient until a time when scientists will be able to thaw the frozen body, cure the disease that caused death and then bring the person back to life.

Already life spans have dramatically increased – for most of the time that the human species has been on the planet life expectancy was about 20 years. Today in many countries it often exceeds 80 years. Scientists are now turning their attention to two of the great mysteries: why do we age, and what can we do about it?

Death is a **paradox**. On the one hand, in the face of over-population, it can be viewed as a terrible necessity; on the other, it adds seriousness and meaning to what we do in life. Death might be seen by some to be a taboo, but worldwide the majority of people do not view it as a tragedy but rather as a part of life. Perhaps, instead of scientists working on the quantity of future life, they would be better employed turning their attention to the quality of present life.

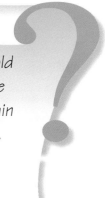

Activity

2 Imagine that medical science allows people to live for hundreds of years. Do you think this is a good or a bad thing? What are the changes that would happen in people's lifetimes, and would you be pleased to be able to live so long?

What do you think

'Let's just go ahead and grow old gracefully and leave room for the next ones coming along. The "Chain of Life" must not be tinkered with. Live and let die! Die and let live!'

Do you agree with this view?

Unemployed

Unemployment: out of work, not having paid employment.

Unemployment is the worst evil, in the sense that the unemployed feel that they have fallen out of the common life... they are unwanted.

(William Temple, Archbishop of Canterbury 1881–1944)

When I first saw unemployed men at close quarters, the thing that horrified and amazed me was to find that many of them were ashamed of being unemployed.

(George Orwell, Author)

AIM

Unemployment is a far larger social problem than official figures suggest. The unit examines the causes of unemployment and the groups which are most likely to experience it.

Unemployment – then and now. There were no state benefits in the 1930s (right). Unemployed men in Merseyside (1985) searching for saleable objects among the waste (below).

A

I KNOW 3 TRADES
I SPEAK 3 LANGUAGES
FOUGHT FOR 3 YEARS
HAVE 3 CHILDREN
AND NO WORK FOR
3 MONTHS
BUT I ONLY WANT
ONE JOB

B Before and after

Throughout the period between the two World Wars, and especially during the 1930s, many people in Britain were unemployed. They suffered because of the great economic depression which affected the United States and most European countries. From the end of the Second World War until the 1960s employment in Britain was high, but from the late 1960s onwards unemployment began to rise sharply. Although the size of the working population has steadily increased there are other factors to be considered.

Competition from overseas manufacturers bankrupted some industries or meant they had to employ fewer workers in order to remain competitive. New technology threatened employment because it meant there was less demand for poorly qualified manual workers and more demand for highly skilled workers. When the economy began to expand again in the 1980s, the unskilled unemployed were needed less and less. Even in skilled employment such as printing, offices, car factories and banks, automation has led to widespread job losses. The computer age has taken over many jobs previously done by workers.

THINK ABOUT

1 Consider and then list as many examples of labour-saving equipment that you can think of **a)** in the home, and **b)** at work.

2 What other examples of industries that have been transformed by automation can you think of?

Another problem came about because of regional differences. Some parts of the country suffered much higher unemployment than others. If there is only one type of industry in a particular area and it goes into decline, the effect can be disastrous. The Midlands was badly affected by the cutbacks in the motor industry and the north-east of England relied heavily on the declining cotton industry. As an industry collapsed the people it employed found themselves without a job, often for the first time in their lives. When one industry declines in an area there is often a knock-on effect with other industries, local shops and services.

Some people are employed in 'casual' or seasonal work. During the summer months, certain industries, especially hotels and tourism, take on additional staff to cope with increased business. However, in the quieter winter months these workers are often laid off. Other people have suffered because of structural changes in their workplace. In recent years, new jobs have mainly been created in services requiring specific skills. It may be difficult for an individual to acquire these new skills because of the cost and availability of training schemes and the drop in income during training.

IN THE NEWS

Jobless depression leads to suicide

UNEMPLOYMENT BLAMED FOR CRIME RISE

JOB LOSS LED TO MARRIAGE BREAKDOWN

Value people for what they are, not what they do!

You want a job? Then get on your bike!

1 What images come to your mind when you see the word 'unemployed'?

2 What pictures do these headlines paint of unemployed people?

3 If you were unemployed for a long period of time, how do you think you would be able to cope? How would unemployment affect your life? Do you think you would be able to use your time and skills in a positive way?

The term 'unemployed' is used to describe people facing different situations. Many people may be out of work for a short amount of time at some point in their lives. Others experience frequent periods of unemployment between jobs, but some face long periods of time without any paid work. In this country it appears that certain groups, particularly older and younger workers, minority ethnic groups and those with few skills and qualifications, are more vulnerable to unemployment (**C**).

The young

School leavers who lack qualifications or skills are particularly vulnerable to unemployment.

Older workers

Some employers tend to be ageist and often jobs are harder to find the older you get.

Minority ethnic groups

Among some ethnic minority groups the unemployment level is much higher than the national average.

The less skilled and unqualified

People without qualifications are far more likely to experience unemployment than well-qualified people.

C Who is vulnerable to unemployment?

Activities

1   Can you think of reasons why people from some ethnic minority groups are likely to experience unemployment? Why do older people have more difficulty in finding paid employment?

2   In pairs, act out a scene where a journalist is interviewing someone who has been unemployed for several years. Decide what particular group the person is from and what sort of questions the interviewer will ask (e.g. How do you spend your time? Do you ever think you won't get another job?) Take it in turn to be the unemployed person and discuss what it feels like to describe your thoughts and feelings.

While many people work in jobs which they think are boring or stressful, this is still seen as preferable to being unemployed. There are many positive aspects of work:

It has been said that someone who loses their job usually goes through a number of phases which are similar to those mourning a death: shock, refusal to accept the situation and even optimism, anxiety, longing for the past and finally, acceptance and hopefully a period of adjustment.

gives identity
A person is often defined by the job that he or she does.

creates relationships
It helps bring a person into contact with other people.

is an activity
When a person works they are obliged to follow regular and purposeful activities outside the home.

helps develop skills
Most occupations give workers the chance to learn new skills.

gives a sense of purpose
It gives a person a sense of belonging to the community and having a part to play in being of use to others.

structures time
The working day is set out – as a contrast leisure time and holidays are appreciated.

as a source of income and control
Most people who earn a living feel they have greater independence and control over their lives.

There is no doubt that long-term unemployment causes psychological and financial problems.

Low morale and poor self-esteem

Depression and suicide

Increase in drug/alcohol abuse

Economic cost to society

unemployment

Lacking a sense of purpose

Family tensions and breakdowns

Having little or no money

Vandalism and crime

Boredom and frustration

Loneliness

D How unemployment can affect the individual and society

THINK ABOUT

3 *Look at* **D** *and try to list the difficulties faced by the unemployed under two columns headed 'Personal' and 'Social'.*

4 *Think about the ways unemployment affects people. What effect do you think unemployment would have on the following people?*

- *A 16 year-old school leaver with good GCSE grades.*
- *A recently married individual in their early twenties.*
- *A single parent with young children.*
- *A married person with a family.*
- *A single person in their mid-fifties.*

The issue of unemployment is not just about losing jobs, it is about creating new jobs; about how to avoid wasting the talents of the unemployed; about giving young people a choice when they complete their education. Although the percentage of the population who are out of work in Britain appears to be falling, in some areas there are still large numbers of unemployed people. Even within regions there are some towns with hardly any unemployment, whereas others have very high levels.

It is important to remember that no society can achieve 100% employment because there will always be some people who:

- are unable to work because of illness;
- do not want to work because they find state benefits sufficient for their needs;
- are out of work through no fault of their own.

Unemployment, for whatever reason, is bad for an individual. Being out of work fills most people with feelings of hopelessness, associated with shame, inferiority, anxiety and despair. No other issue affects the quality of life of ordinary people as much as unemployment does.

A life in the day of James Metier

'I usually get up at about eight o'clock. It's the hardest part of the day, but you have to maintain some sort of discipline or you've had it. If you get up too late one day then it throws you out of synch and you end up living at night, which isn't that much of a laugh when you don't have enough money to go out and heating the place costs almost as much.

The idea that people are "well off" on the dole is a myth. You won't starve, but it's still only survival, not living. Once up, I make breakfast: coffee if the money has just come, tea if it hasn't, and some toast.

Unemployment Benefit Attendance Card! **UB40z**

SURNAME	*METIER J*	INITIALS	NI NUMBER

1 Important Notes About Claiming Benefit

- **If you wish to continue claiming** unemployment benefit and/or supplementary allowance because you are unemployed please sign at the Unemployment Benefit Office on the days-and at the times shown on the right. Please bring this card.

- **You could lose benefit** if you do not claim on the day shown. If you cannot claim on this day go to the Unemployment Benefit Office the very next day you can.

- **If you start work** or a training scheme, or if you claim another benefit, fill in parts 2 and 3 of this card and post it. (It can be folded and stuck down.) If you become unemployed again you should claim benefit on your first day of unemployment.

- **If you are in doubt on any point, ask us for advice.**

Please come in on

Then next on

And then every week on

(day)

TIME

BOX

Down the library

Then it's down to the warmth of the library for the papers. At the library there's a lot of us about, although we never let on that we're in the same boat. Being registered unemployed is still seen as a self-inflicted disability. In the 1930s it was apparently different; a lot of collective hanging around on street corners; comradeship in poverty. Nowadays we've got television and the man standing in front of you in the queue at the Unemployment isn't anything to do with you.

Doing the shopping

After going through all the likely jobs in the national papers (which takes about 45 seconds) it's off down to the shops for bread, milk, fresh vegetables and 25p worth of cheese. It's amazing how some shopkeepers look at you as if you've just crawled out from underneath the arches when you ask for half a pound of carrots. Others though are great and slip in an extra potato without making out they've just given you the world. Generally, I like shopping. I've also taken up cooking in a big way since I stopped work.

Carpentry classes

On the way back from the shops I pick up the local paper and go through the Sits Vac over a bowl of soup. After "lunch" if it's a Monday or a Wednesday I go to a carpentry class at the local Adult Education Centre. These courses are free if you're signing on. They won't give you a trade but it's better than the alternative – Nothing.

A sort of daze

The important thing when you're on the dole is to keep doing things. When I was first made redundant I went round in a sort of daze for about a month. It was as if I had no rhythm. That machine I'd always complained about had been like a life support system and without it I collapsed. I used to sit on the sofa all day watching soaps until I felt them coming up in the back of my throat.

Once you get caught up in this trap you go numb; all your emotions, except useless ones like self-pity, seem to pack in. You sink very fast without even realising it. After the initial shock of losing your job and the indignity of signing on your self-respect is in tatters. It's hardly surprising; since the day that you started work you've been defined by society and by yourself by the work you do. Suddenly, you do nothing. Therefore…

In truth it's a false equation but it's one that takes an almost total shift in your way of seeing things to disprove it.

Planned pattern

The thing is to establish some kind of planned pattern on the day. If you don't give your life a structure then the whole thing falls to pieces.

So, if there are no classes in the afternoons I go for walks if the weather's all right, or read. The time goes quickly if you set yourself tasks and then do them but it hangs very heavy if you just pick at things haphazardly. You end up watching the kettle boil just for something to do.

Cooking the supper

About six o'clock I start preparing the big meal of the day. I take a lot of time over it even though I've at last got to the stage where I can cook at least two different vegetables in two different saucepans without the potatoes coming out like bits of hard-core and the cabbage like a damp flannel. The meal is usually a variation of cauliflower cheese (a good protein-packed feast for under a pound) or an apology for spaghetti bolognaise.

Laughter and anger

After supper we talk or read or play a board game. Every other Friday we go out for exactly two drinks each or alternatively to the cinema. I don't watch much television but I do enjoy those programmes when they interview some MP and he or she tells you how sorry they are about the unemployment but how the country must keep swallowing the medicine for its own good. It's important to watch these things because they produce two emotions which are essential to my survival: laughter and anger. Usually at about 10.30 we turn off the trusty gas heater and go to bed.'

What do you think ?

The article was written in the 1980s but the effects of unemployment remain the same.

'People are valued for what they do, not who they are.' How can we change this view?

Violence

Violence: the unlawful exercise of physical force. In other words, unacceptable behaviour which gives rise to injury or upset.

It is society's tolerance of violence in society that's probably responsible for violent behaviour more than any motion picture or television show.

(Clint Eastwood, Actor)

Keep violence in the mind where it belongs.

(Brian Aldiss, Science fiction writer)

AIM In this unit we will be examining the nature of violence in today's society and ask if the role of the media and film industry encourages violence or helps us to understand it.

Almost every day there is a report in the media about a violent incident or attack. From all over the world we hear stories of riots, shootings, war, murder, rape, and torture. If you include the wider meanings of the word 'violence', such as cruelty to animals and the destruction of the environment, it appears to be one of the main characteristics of the human race.

Throughout the twentieth century, the media seem intent on 'proving' that our society is becoming more and more violent. In the public mind, the rising crime figures and horrific, well publicised mass murders such as Hungerford and Dunblane, appear to support claims that a wave of violence has society in its grip. In the past it has been difficult to establish whether crime rates are true indicators supporting this belief. The problem stems mainly from the 'dark figure' of unreported crime (**A**).

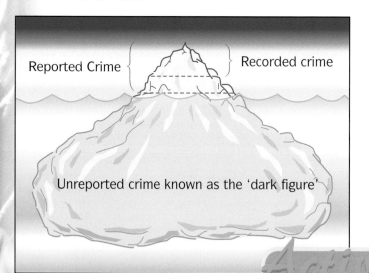

Reported Crime   Recorded crime

Unreported crime known as the 'dark figure'

 A The 'dark figure'

Activities

1 What sort of violent crimes do you think would go unreported?

2 What is the difference between reported and recorded crime?

3 Which of the following crimes do you think are the most serious. Explain your choices:

Shoplifting   Vandalism   Fraud   Burglary   Murder

Rape   Drug dealing

When faced with rising crime figures, some experts assure us that statistics can be misleading, that violence in Britain is not commonplace. They are quick to point out that vicious crimes such as murder and rape are now recorded more closely than in the past. They do not necessarily occur more often. Compared with the rest of the world, England and Wales have a low homicide rate. Analysis of homicides in Britain during the 1990s, however, reveal some disturbing patterns. Most at risk from violent death are babies, followed by men aged 16–49 years, frequently through drunken fights and drug related incidents. Domestic disputes are the most common cause of violent death. In the late 1990s an average number of 80 under-16 year-olds were murdered every year. Sixty of these were killed by close relatives, 10 by extended family members and 10 by strangers.

Without doubt, poverty, oppression and deprivation often promote violent behaviour but trying to identify the root causes of violent crime is an extremely difficult task because there are so many and they are often inter-related. The media are accused, not only for being irresponsible with sensational headlines, but also for portraying 'dangerous role models' who can have a disturbing effect on young people who may be more likely to commit crime.

Even research into the roots of violence does not provide a clear, agreed answer.

Television
Internet
Press **Books** MUSIC
ADVERTISING
Childhood experiences
Jealousy Ignorance
HUMILIATION
WAR
Unemployment
Protest
Drugs/alcohol
POVERTY

IN THE NEWS

THUGS WHO IMPERSONATE THE BIG-SCREEN

The end to soccer violence

Britain 'not violent' according to Prime Minister

Hollywood must shut down its nightmare factory

Domestic violence is on the increase!

B The roots of violence

THINK ABOUT

1 In small groups, try to think of other possible 'roots of violence'.

2 Which one, in your group's opinion, is the most powerful influence?

3 Generally speaking, women and girls seem to be less involved in violence than men and boys. Why do you think this is?

4 Mohondas Gandhi, a political and spiritual leader in India once said: 'Poverty is the worst kind of violence'. What do you think he meant by this?

'Shoot!'   **C**

Activity

4 Look at the cartoon (**C**). Can you think of examples of:
a) words which have an aggressive meaning?
b) words which can be misused in an aggressive way?

From an early age, many of us are brought up to believe that competition is a good thing. In many sports, for example, we are taught 'no pain no gain', that 'winning is everything' and tough or aggressive competitors are to be admired. Sometimes though, the wish to win becomes more important than anything else, and a sport can become dishonest and violent.

There is clearly a fine dividing line between aggression and violence. Aggression in humans serves some positive functions as we need to stand up for ourselves and compete against others. We sometimes use language in an aggressive way. We talk about 'tackling a problem' or 'attacking with a will to win'. Unfortunately, aggression can easily spill over into violence which is threatening, destructive and intentional.

Increasingly in films and books the violence of the wicked is balanced by the violence of the good. Even William Shakespeare's work contains many violent scenes: his play called 'Titus Andronicus' has been criticised as 'depraved porno-violent material', and is unlikely to be seen again on stage or adapted for television. Other books have been criticised for inciting violence in some of its readers. The man who killed the ex-Beatle, John Lennon, was obsessed with the hero of J D Salinger's book, *Catcher In The Rye*. The individual who attempted to assassinate Ronald Reagan when he was President of the United States, had the same book in his possession. Also it was suggested that he had been acting out a fantasy inspired by the violent film *Taxi Driver*.

Neither are the music and fashion worlds free from blame. In 1997, a band called The Prodigy released a single entitled 'Smack My Bitch Up'. It was claimed by some critics that the words and accompaning video incited violence against women. The banning of the Prodigy's video, however, immediately led to increased album sales! In a similar way, the clothes group Benetton was severely criticised and forced to withdraw posters which glorified violence. This only increased interest and sales! Both examples made use of well known shock tactics in order to shake things up, at the same time proving the old saying, 'There is no such thing as bad publicity'.

In recent years certain horrific crimes appear to reinforce the belief that screen violence may influence violent behaviour, as some people may consider copying what they watch. It has been suggested that the child murderers of the toddler James Bulger were influenced by the video *Child's Play 3*. The film was also linked to the savage killing of a 16 year-old Manchester girl. Some researchers believe, however, that it is not violent videos that make young people violent, it is just a trend for violence that makes them enjoy watching violent videos. In other words, these young people do not learn violence from films: they are violent already. What is clearly disturbing is that, from viewing, people learn about and attempt to imitate a style of violence.

We like to believe that only inadequate people resort to violence but everywhere we look in the media, we receive the opposite message. Some regard violent people as exciting, powerful and glamorous. If there is no other way to make your mark in the world, violence can turn you into somebody. It is often suggested that people who commit acts of violence are acting like animals. This is misleading because violence within the same animal species only occurs in unusual circumstances of food shortage, over-population or self-defence. Humans are uniquely cruel and violent. When murder or violent behaviour occurs, humans are behaving only like humans and not like any other living creature.

The cult of violence?   **D**

VIOLENCE IN THE MEDIA

FOR

Sensitisation?
This process makes people more sensitive to the sufferings of victims of violence.

Catharsis?
Viewing violence can rid people of violent emotions and impulses.

AGAINST

De-sensitisation?
The more we view violent acts, the more we become immune to the suffering caused by violence.

Disinhibition?
People become more inclined to commit violent acts.

The 'violence debate'   **E**

Activities

5   Why do horror films/videos, full of violence and terror, attract such large audiences?

6   Choose one of the following activities.
   a) Compare two different newspapers of the same date. Look through them carefully to find any reference to reported incidents of violence. Note down the type of language used in the articles.
   b) Choose two television programmes (one factual, one fictional) which contain some violent incidents/scenes and describe how they were portrayed.

What do you think

Look carefully at the different viewpoints set out in the diagram (**E**). Which one do you agree with most?

War

War: a period of armed conflict between two or more countries, normally lasting over 24 hours.

When you go home, tell them of us and say, 'For your tomorrows, these gave their today'.

(John Maxwell Edmonds 1875–1958)

*Through these fields of destruction
Baptisms of fire
I've witnessed your suffering
As the battle raged higher.*

(Mark Knopfler, singer/guitarist)

AIM This unit highlights the ways in which modern warfare, apart from causing deaths and injuries, inflicts suffering on a far wider scale.

Since the beginning of history, people have fought against other people. Any struggle in which two large groups try to destroy one another is a war. When armies were quite small, few people were involved in the politics of war. Unless a country was invaded civilians did not even feel the effects of war. Nowadays, wars always cause suffering and hardship and leave destruction behind them.

From an early age, we are taught that we must learn from the mistakes of history. Unfortunately, no one appears to learn from the brutality and devastation of warfare. More people have died in wars this century than all the other wars throughout history. Today, despite the use of modern weaponry such as laser guided missiles, military activity is not confined to the combatants. The lives of millions of innocent victims are affected by warfare, whereas in the past there were hardly any civilian casualties. In the Second World War 25 million people died in the armed services, but a further 35 million civilians died as a result of this global war.

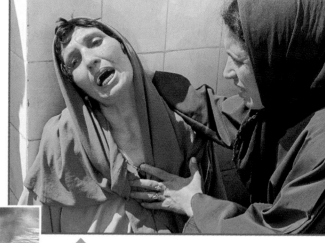

A Images of war

THINK ABOUT

1 *What do these two photos (**A**) tell us about the 'innocent victims' of war?*

In this day and age very few nations or groups choose to go to war if they can achieve their aims peacefully. Fighting only starts when a nation wants something so much that it is willing to risk everything to get it. Basically the important reasons for many of the violent struggles in the world can be listed under five catergories:

War for wealth

Wars in the past were often fought for this reason. A nation would attempt to seize the property of another, not intending to force people off their land, rather just to collect taxes from the invaded peoples.

War for territory

Sometimes wars were fought because people preferred the horrors of war to the hardships of poverty. Through invasion people could have more land which in turn allowed them to grow more to eat and to prosper.

War for power or foreign domination

Some wars have been fought by nations in order to gain or increase their power. Often the conflict succeeds in strengthening the government and uniting the people.

War for religious or political belief

Some countries find themselves in conflict with other nations because of differences in religious or political beliefs. Some of the fiercest struggles taking place in the world today are due to religious motivation.

War for security

A nation may keep its armed forces on standby for self defence. On occasions, it may decide to strike the first blow or it may attack a weaker neighbouring country, thereby creating a buffer zone.

It is rare when there is a single, clear cause for the outbreak of war and the fault is very rarely just on one side. Wars have been fought out of fear, protest against injustice, and because of the actions of corrupt governments or evil individuals. All kinds of historical factors go into the situation but the result in each case is the same: loss of life, destruction, mental and physical suffering, enormous debts and a huge refugee problem.

THINK ABOUT

2 'I think of how many times I used to wonder how scared and homesick you must have been in that strange country called Vietnam… But this I know. I would rather to have had you for 21 years, and all the pain that goes with losing you, than never to have had you at all.'

What does this tell you about those involved in war?

IN THE NEWS

A MOTHER IN TORMENT

Peace in flames

Echoes of the holocaust

SOLDIERS FOR SALE

Boy soldiers taught to murder and rape

1 Can you think of any films/programmes about war which:
a) make war out to be heroic/romantic?
b) try to give a more realistic picture of war?

2 What are some of the main causes of conflict between: family, friends, neighbours, different cultures, nations? Write down at least two causes under each heading.

3 What is the meaning behind the headline 'Echoes of the holocaust'?

Despite the fact that millions of lives have been affected by warfare some people clearly believe that war can be justified in self defence, to fight oppression, or to put right injustice. Others adopt a pacifist response believing that it is wrong to fight under any circumstances. Others are happy to judge the morality of each war by applying a set of rules or 'conditions' of war.

Conditions for a just war

1 War cannot be started by an individual. It must be declared by the highest authority in the land (i.e. the **sovereign** or government).

2 There must be a just cause. In practice this can only happen when a country is defending itself from an aggressor.

3 It must be a last resort. In other words every means of resolving the dispute peacefully must have been tried.

4 The war has a clear and just aim and all fighting must stop once this has been achieved.

5 More good than evil must be expected to come out of the war. No matter how just the cause, the 'cost' of going to war may be too high a price to pay.

6 The war must be waged in a just way. The safety of non-combatants should be ensured and limits placed on the amount of force necessary to achieve the objectives.

7 There must be a reasonable chance of success. It would be wrong to lose thousands of lives, knowing there was no chance of winning.

THINK ABOUT

3 *People are divided over whether there can be such a thing as a 'just war'. What do you think? In small groups, discuss the following questions:*

a) What was the main reason for condition one above?

b) Think of two examples in the twentieth century which you think agree with condition two.

c) Is it always possible to meet condition three?

4 *An old African Proverb states that, 'When two elephants fight, it is always the grass that gets trampled'. What do you think this means?*

5 *Read the comment below by Saioh Camara, a boy who enlisted in the army at the age of 12 in Sierra Leone's bloody civil war:*

'The first time I killed I did not worry about it. In fact, I felt happy because I had been alone and feeling bored.'

What is your reaction to what he is saying?

The victims of war **B**

Several disturbing practices have become more common in war. In Africa, thousands of young children, sometimes aged as young as eight years, are being forced into armies to fight in civil wars.

Rival armies in the Balkans, intent on crushing one another quite often deliberately target civilians. They recklessly use landmines and refugees are terrorised by the opposing groups. We increasingly hear the term 'ethnic cleansing', the modern day phrase for mass murder or genocide. As old feuds rise to the surface **atrocities** are increasingly reported and even United Nations peacekeeping forces and Red Cross helpers are not exempt from such brutality. Today, in Cambodia, evidence of the horrors inflicted under Pol Pot's murderous leadership from 1975 to 1978 is still being found in the 'killing fields'. Nobody in this once beautiful country escaped the loss of a family member whether through torture, execution, starvation or disease.

Today, the threat of world war is unlikely because of the devastation that would be created by the use of nuclear weaponry. This does not mean, however, that wars no longer take place.

Everyday, somewhere in the world, people are being killed in armed conflicts. It would be fair to say that very few wars, from the times of the Crusades through to modern day conflicts, could honestly be described as 'just' wars. We have to bear in mind, however, that even the great pacifist, Mohondas Gandhi, recognised that sometimes to go to war was morally better than to do nothing in the face of evil.

Activities

1 Do you think the seven conditions can be applied to a modern day conflict? Give reasons for your answer.

2 Choose any war to research, and using the seven 'conditions' decide whether or not the war can be described as just.

3 These two illustrations (**C**) are symbols of peace. Design your own symbol for an agency working for international peace. Explain why you have drawn your particular design and what it represents.

C Symbols of peace

What do you think

'Guilt rests not only with those who pulled the trigger but also with those who winked as it happened.'

(Robert J Brodey)

Explain what you think Brodey means in his comment above?

X-rated

X-rated: a classification of material as suitable for adults only.

We can't have freedom for adults in this country because we can't trust adults to protect children.

(David Ferman, Film censor and Ex-Director of the BBFC)

It's simple. PG means the hero gets the girl, 15 means the villain gets the girl and 18 means everybody gets the girl.

(Michael Douglas, Actor)

AIM

The unit examines the historical background to censorship in relation to films and asks whether, in a modern technological age, the censor still has a role to play.

If a sign says 'No Smoking' or '30 MPH speed limit' some people will deliberately ignore it. If a book is censored we will try and get copies of it. When certain songs or albums are banned from public broadcast the result is normally increased sales. A lot of people believe that censorship denies us one of our most valued rights – the freedom of choice. There are three kinds of censorship, two of which are straightforward: **personal** and **commercial**.

We all exercise personal censorship by our choices. Whether we buy a CD or not, whether we watch a television programme or not is a personal choice. Commercial censorship happens because, whether we like it or not, big business promotes books, films and goods that bring in money. Things that do not make profits quickly get frozen out. Ironically, the first film to be censored in Britain was in 1898 and starred a piece of Stilton cheese! *Cheese Mites* was filmed under a microscope and magnified over 100 times. The British Cheese Federation managed to get the documentary film banned on the grounds that the bacterial movement seen under the microscope could put off potential customers.

The main problem lies with the third catergory, **reference** censorship. This occurs when a recognised authority decides what is good for us, what we can read or buy and in the case of films, watch.

Activities

1 What is the meaning of the word 'censorship'?

2 Explain in your own words what is meant by 'personal', 'commerical' and 'reference' censorship. Can you think of examples of the three categories?

Most films were first viewed in amusement parks, fairs and arcades but between 1906 and 1916 over 3,600 purpose built cinemas sprang up across Britain. There were concerns expressed about the safety of these cinemas so local authorities licenced them. Safety was the main concern but soon the authorities extended their licence to control the sorts of films being shown. To get round this problem the movie industry asked the government to appoint a censorship board but this request was turned down. In response, the industry set up its own board in 1912 – the British Board of Film Censors (BBFC). Initially all films were reviewed with only two taboos in mind: nudity and representations of Christ.

Ever since the birth of the film industry people have been concerned that what we see and hear influences the way we behave. Without doubt certain individuals are more vulnerable to serious harm than others. Young children, for example, are especially at risk.

Originally the authorities were concerned that the cinema seemed to threaten social order: they feared it could give people bad ideas or even spark off revolutions. Certain films were banned because they contained dangerous images, for example stressing the contrast between rich and poor. In 1926 Sergei Eisenstein's classic *Battleship Potemkin* was banned because it portrayed revolutionary activities. It was finally passed and given a certificate in 1954. The first vampire film *Nosferatu* in 1922 met with a similar fate and in 1933 the Board introduced for the first time the 'H' Certificate in response to the horror film *Frankenstein*. In the early 1930s a ruling was made that film scripts had to be submitted before the film could be made. Censors rejected scripts that contained too much swearing, sexual immorality or too much of 'the tragic and **sordid** side of poverty'.

The Second World War saw a change mainly brought about by Pathé Newsreel documentaries on the brutality of concentration camps. These films were not submitted to the censor. If they had been they would have been X-rated and one doubts whether the general public would have ever witnessed the horrific film evidence of the Nazi holocaust.

After 1945 films began to look at different subjects, such as social problems and sex. Two films released in 1954 caused major headaches for the censorship board. *The Wild One* starring Marlon Brando was banned for over 14 years before it was certificated. It was described as a 'spectacle of unbridled hooliganism'. *The Blackboard Jungle* was passed for viewing but the soundtrack, 'Rock Around the Clock' by Bill Haley and the Comets – according to media reports – caused 'riots and fights' in the audiences. In 1956, a new 'X' Certificate was introduced preventing under 18s from viewing certain movies.

During the 1960s and 1970s the main concerns of the censors were threefold: politics, religion and sex. The release of two films in 1971, *Straw Dogs* and *A Clockwork Orange*, introduced a need for a fourth concern, sexual violence. The X-rated film could now only be viewed by over 18s but technology was about to undermine the whole system. By 1980 the launch of the home video recorder meant that censorship by age had almost disappeared. Suddenly, only parents stood between children and the worst excesses of films. Surveys revealed that few parents took their role seriously.

A *Nosferatu – banned!*

THINK ABOUT

1 Within groups brainstorm what should or should not be allowed to be shown on television or in the cinema.

2 Should there be restrictions on what time of day certain news items can be shown on television? Do you think that sometimes there are good reasons for censorship?

IN THE NEWS

Video 'nasties' banned to protect the young

Film blamed for murders

CENSORSHIP SHOULD BE IN THE HOME

1 What dangers are being highlighted in these headlines?

Hooking of the video junkies

2 Act out or discuss a scene between a parent who thinks there is too much violence in programmes or films and a producer who insists they only reflect real life. Refer to the arguments in the unit on Violence (**E**). The producer might claim that documentaries and the news contains violence all the time. The parent might be worried about messages in cartoons or certain films.

Horror is invading the home

The new video technology evaded controls: the only law which could be used was the 'depraved and corrupt test' of obscene publications under the Criminal Law Act 1977. The problem created by video rental was twofold: firstly, the popularity of the video was blamed for the closure of hundreds of cinemas nationwide; secondly, videos were not censored and thousands of horror movies and 'video nasties' were freely available to any age group. In 1983 the film classifications of X, A and U were replaced with a wider spread of categories, U, 12, 15, PG and 18. In 1984 the government responded to public worries with the Video Recordings Act which for the first time legally enforced censorship.

Films that have raised concerns about 'audience impact'

In August 1987 there was a public outcry when the film *Rambo* was blamed in part for the murder of 14 people in Hungerford. The film *Child's Play 3* was said to have been a factor in other murders. In 1994 the film *Natural Born Killers* was accused of causing real life copycat killings in the United States. Whatever the truth behind the accusations new laws controlling the sale and rental of violent videos were proposed in the main to protect children. The Criminal Justice and Public Order Act of 1994 established that a video would be judged by introducing strict new criteria under which films would be classified. The video would be judged with special regard to:

a) criminal behaviour;
b) illegal drugs;
c) violent behaviour or incident;
d) horrific behaviour or incidents;
e) human sexual activity.

In addition, the Act extended the definition of video recording to any device capable of storing data electronically. In practice, this system is not foolproof.

Authorised censors can control films and tapes that physically have to pass through their hands but what about the future? What happens now that telephone lines and computer modems join cable and satellite to bypass the censors. These delivery systems for home entertainment will make regulation difficult. As virtual reality will merge with the Net, interactive television and video games will undoubtedly become more sophisticated, and the censors will face an impossible task.

Technology is outstripping the ability of censors to do their job. The proposed V-chip – which allows domestic censorship of television programmes – may offer some continued protection to children but many believe that reference censorship will become extinct. In the past the main debate was always whether material should be censored. In the future, the question will focus on how to teach children to live in an uncensorable world.

Activities

3 What do you think about the suggestion that violent videos can influence the behaviour of some people?

4 Is it fair to ban certain films because of the effect they might have on a few people?

C The future?

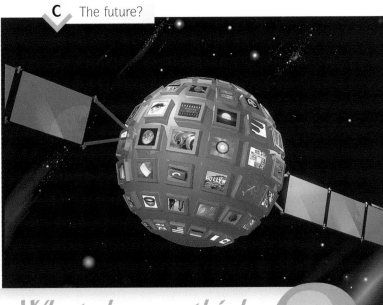

What do you think

In an interview, when asked about uncensorable technology, a film critic replied, 'Becoming a "traffic cop on the information highway" will not be easy!' How might these technological advances change our viewing in the future? Has the issue of censorship been driven from the authorities into the family and if so, is this a good thing?

STALLONE is back as... RAMBO FIRST BLOOD PART II

No man, no law, no war can stop him.

Youth

Youth: describes the period between childhood and adult age.

Come mothers and fathers
Throughout the land
And don't criticise
What you don't understand

(Bob Dylan, Poet and singer)

Adolescents turn on you –
that's their job.

(Ron Howard, Actor/Director)

AIM This section examines the development of youth cultures over the last 50 years and highlights the problems which can be caused by the so-called 'generation gap'.

Life can be difficult when you are a teenager: 'You feel weird, your friends are weirder and your body does weirder things still'. Little wonder that the world at this age confuses so many and appears to be chaotic. It is a time of change, when individuals begin to leave the dependent world of the child and enter the adult world. There are several key stages in this transition:

- leaving education and entering employment;
- becoming increasingly independent of the family;
- becoming involved in adult activities such as drinking, driving and having sex;
- increasing status in society.

In normal life we form friendships with other people with whom we have something in common. Young people in particular feel happy and secure in a group. Problems can arise when one group misunderstands another, or feels that it has been unfairly singled out. It is easy for one group to generalise about another: old people are 'boring' or 'past it', while young people 'don't know what hard work is'. This type of stereotyping helps reinforce the 'generation gap'.

Today it is not easy to determine when youth begins and ends. Children are growing up much more quickly in terms of their attitudes and expectations.

Childhood – Tweenhood – Adolescence

In the United States, for example, the term 'tweenhood' is increasingly used to describe children between childhood and adolescence (aged 8–12 years). The 'tweens' have turned their backs on the traditional children's past-times. Instead they pursue fashion and style. Busy parents are blamed for spending less time with their children, so television, magazines and peers are increasingly important in the children's lives.

Without doubt improved diets and rising standards of living have also accelerated children's physical and sexual development.

An individual's legal rights increase as they go through the teenage years until children are no longer regarded as 'minors' but have reached the age of 'majority'. In Britain at the age of 18 years people are regarded as adults. They are allowed to vote, marry, give blood and to sit on juries.

The law states that…

From 5 years
- you must have a full-time education.

From 10 years
- you can be convicted of a crime.

From 12 years
- you can buy a pet.

From 13 years
- you can get a part-time job but with certain restrictions.

From 14 years
- you can go into a pub, but cannot buy or drink alcohol.

From 15 years
- you can watch a category 15 film.

From 16 years
- you can leave school and work full-time.
- you can marry with your parents'/guardians' consent.

From 17 years
- you can hold a driving licence.

From 18 years
- you are an adult.
- you can vote in elections.

Despite being able to drive and fight for their country at 17 years and legally allowed to be sexually active at 16, parents still have custody over their children until they reach 18 years. Many young people, however, continue to be dependent on their parents into their twenties. Some remain living at home because of housing costs and job shortages. In addition, parents are often expected to contribute financially if their child follows a college or university course.

The separation of the adult world of responsibilities and work and the childhood world of play has only really occurred over the last few hundred years. History books record the ill fated Children's Crusade in 1212 said to involve 30,000 children who set off to fight in the Holy Land. They failed to reach their destination and thousands were sold into slavery. In the Middle Ages children dressed as adults and were expected to work and join in grown-up activities. By the eighteenth century, children over the age of four were expected to work and apprenticeships started between the ages of seven and twelve years. In Western societies it was the development of education that was to be one of the main factors in changing the status of children. In some cultures today the change to adulthood takes place much earlier, with no period of youth. This occurs especially in developing countries where children are expected to fend for themselves or work to support their families.

 A Children grew up quickly in the past

THINK ABOUT

1 *The age at which countries allow young people to marry varies. Do you think Britain is wrong to set the minimum age at 16 (with the permission of parents)? At what age do you think young people should be allowed to get married?*

2 *'You should be able to leave school earlier than 16 if you want to.' 'People aged 18 are too young and inexperienced to sit on juries.' Do you agree or disagree with these statements, and for what reasons?*

B The images of youth

Many observers believe that the real development of 'youth subculture' began after the Second World War. The word 'culture' refers to the values, attitudes and way of life of people in a society. 'Subculture' refers to a way of life which puts certain members outside the system. Within any one society there may be a variety of subcultures which differ in ways such as language, interests and appearance. Youth subcultures often have their own particular style of dress and music which sets them apart from others.

The 1950s and 1960s witnessed this spread of youth subculture as young people associated with changing attitudes and the development of modern music. The record industry, television and magazine publishers quickly realised the value of targeting the younger generations. The manufacturing industries, particularly the fashion world, also saw opportunities to sell to this new generation. The mass media were not slow in reporting these new, 'way out' styles and helped to transmit new trends and ideas to the young. All these changes gave rise to a large number of youth subcultures, some of which reflect specific social class, ethnic and gender differences.

During the early 1960s reports of clashes between 'mods' and 'rockers' were commonplace and each group was clearly identified by what they wore and drove. Mods rode scooters, had short hair and wore smart suits and parkas. Rockers preferred motorbikes, long hair, leather jackets and jeans. Newspapers often overdramatised stories of these clashes describing them as 'riots' or 'battles'. The public urged on by the media, became increasingly concerned. Finally it became apparent that as the media painted a picture of so-called troublemakers, they in turn tried to live up to their 'reputation'.

By the mid 1960s, parents often regarded the younger generation as a threat to their way of life. Experimental drug use and fashion trends helped to reinforce this 'generation gap'. Many young people adopted the lifestyle of 'hippies'. They were intelligent and politically very aware. 'Flower power', 'Ban the Bomb' and anti-Vietnam War protests were common and found support in the music industry. People like Bob Dylan and Jimi Hendrix, or groups such as The Beatles and The Rolling Stones were influential in setting trends. The slogan adopted by the hippies was 'Turn on, Tune in and Drop out', a clear reference to drugs and rejecting the 'rat-race' of the career ladder.

The 'flower power' era

Activities

Write a list of the advantages and disadvantages of being young.

1   Explain the difference between a 'culture' and a 'subculture'.

2   Describe how the lifestyle of any one youth subculture discussed in this unit set it apart from the rest of society.

IN THE NEWS

The young have it easy

The younger generation – all rights and no responsibilities!

A law unto themselves

ALL WORK AND NO PLAY IN THE STRESSFUL NINETIES

Tomorrow belongs to us

1   What sort of images do these headlines portray of young people today? Which one do you disagree with most? Give reasons for your choice.

2   How do you think older generations view young people today?

Each following decade saw new youth subcultures and the press continued to exaggerate the problems caused by them: in the early 1970s the media created worries about the intimidating behaviour of the skinheads with their shaved heads and 'bovver' boots. In the late 1970s, the punks deliberately set out to shock the public. This began as a working class subculture of a generation hit by unemployment. Their slogans of 'No future' and 'No wealth' were seen as a reaction against the rich or the ruling classes. Ripped T-shirts, wearing of Nazi swastikas and anti-social behaviour helped to build a disturbing image but in reality, the fashion and music worlds often cleverly manufactured and promoted the 'image'.

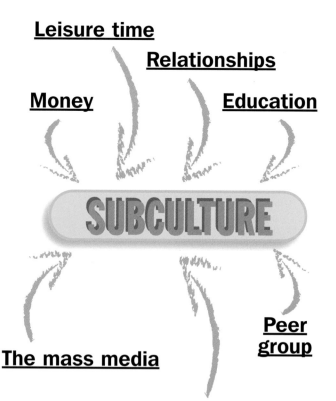

Leisure time

Relationships

Money

Education

SUBCULTURE

The mass media

Peer group

Fashion trends

D   The creation of a subculture

By the end of the 1980s, however, the media began to paint a portrait of an increasingly responsible generation. Stability in marriage and family, previously seen as unfashionable by the youth of the 1960s and 1970s, was now regarded as desirable. The vast majority were looking for long-term stable relationships and job security.

The media rarely depict young people as success stories: it is more likely to be about stress, children on the street, in trouble, or failing exams. Some teenagers do have serious problems, and many young people today have grown up in broken homes. As teenagers try to establish their own identity they often relate to a particular youth culture. This can serve a useful purpose as it can help them through a period of stress and uncertainty. The vast majority of young individuals manage to cope with things, enjoy life and grow up to be well balanced adults.

Activities

3 Young people in the 1990s have been described as belonging to a 'designer subculture'. What do you think is meant by this description? How would you describe the 'subculture' of young people today?

4 Belonging to particular groups or gangs often causes arguments between parents and children.
a) Make a list of the things they might quarrel about.
b) In pairs, choose some of these arguments and develop role plays that show two different ways of handling the problem so that it:
  i) is sorted out, or
  ii) remains unresolved.

5 Role-play a scene where a parent tries to give advice to a teenage son or daughter about the way they dress and the people they go around with. Take it in turns to be the parent and the teenager.

The new generation – increasingly responsible? **E**

What do you think ?

'The 1990s was just an era of imitation – clothes, music, everything!' Do you agree?

Zero

'Homeless, Hungry, Help Me' cards everywhere. But that doesn't hide the pain, the suffering, the awfulness of sleeping on the streets. The dreadful feeling of not being as good as the people walking by. The terrifying fear of another, yet another night hiding in a corner hoping you won't be noticed, hoping you don't matter but praying you do.

(Anonymous poet in Crisis News)

Zero: the lowest point, having no value.

If you don't have a home, it makes it even harder to get a job. If you don't have a job, your options for housing are extremely limited.

(Michael Duncan – *The Big Issue*)

AIM The unit examines the causes of homelessness and the ways in which several housing charities are attempting to help and at the same time offer possible solutions.

The problem of homelessness can be witnessed on the streets of cities, and even small towns. No one knows how many people are homeless in the world and estimates range from 100 million to two billion. Every day in Britain thousands of people end up sleeping rough. Some people choose this way of life but the majority end up in this situation through little fault of their own. Being cold, hungry and homeless is not a situation many people would wish to be in.

IN THE NEWS

NOWHERE TO GO, NO ONE TO CARE

1 Think about what the word 'home' means to you. List all your ideas.

NO HOME, NO HOPE!

2 Make a list of as many things as possible which are good and not so good about living at home.

The dangers of the streets

In Britain today, being homeless means you are worth zero!

3 The following well known phrases and expressions all contain the word 'home'. Read each phrase and consider:

a) what each one means;

b) what image of 'home' each phrase brings to your mind.

4 In your opinion, which groups in society are most likely to end up being homeless?

HOME SWEET HOME

HOMELESS

Make yourself at home

HOMESICK

Many homeless people are forced to beg, live on the streets or sleep rough in shop doorways. Being homeless means not having a roof over your head. A 'home' however, is more than just a roof over one's head. A Church of England report, 'Faith in the City', defines what a home is:

> A home is more than having a roof over one's head. Decent housing certainly means a place that is dry and warm and in reasonable repair. It also means security, privacy, sufficient space, a place where people can grow and make choices.
>
> 'Faith in the City'

During the 1990s, the lack of decent, secure and affordable housing combined with benefit cuts to 16 and 17 year-olds saw the problem of homelessness among single people growing. Many ended up sleeping rough on the streets and the statistics were alarming: Over 90% were male, over 50% drank heavily, roughly 30% were mentally ill and about 15% were dependent on illegal drugs. To earn money some individuals beg and others turn to crime and prostitution, exposing themselves to great dangers.

Most people realise that the homeless problem is far worse than the official government statistics suggest: many 'unofficial' homeless people are left out of the figures. Single people and childless couples are not entitled to housing under the homelessness laws and so are not included in official statistics. Such people may be in hostels, bed and breakfasts, sleeping rough, squatting or being put up by friends.

THINK ABOUT

1 In pairs draft a letter to your local newspaper expressing your concern about the plight of the homeless in your area. Suggest what you think could be done to help them.

2 In groups, discuss the 'Faith in the City' definition. What is the difference between a 'house' and a 'home'?

Family arguments   Looking for work

Mentally ill   Divorce   Debt and eviction

HOMELESS

Need for independence   Addiction

People who slip through the 'support network'

Family breakup   Physical/sexual abuse

Not all the homeless are unemployed but the jobs that some manage to find are often very poorly paid. Finding a job though is almost impossible because most employers will not consider a person for a job unless they can give a home address.

A common view is that people are homeless through their own fault. Many are shocked to learn the homeless are not all drunks, beggars, mentally ill or drug addicts. People become homeless for a variety of reasons; many are just the victims of bad luck, often caused by the breakdown of marriages or job loss.

 A   The main reasons why people end up homeless

THINK ABOUT

3 *Working in groups, look at figure **A** and discuss the various reasons why so many people become homeless. Which do you think are the main reasons? Make a note of your conclusions. Are the reasons why young people become homeless different from the reasons why older people become homeless?*

4 *Homeless people are deprived of many things that we take for granted. Make a list of these in order of importance.*

5 *People walk past you and think, 'Homelessness, it's bad but it's there', instead of thinking, 'It's there and it's bad'. Does your group agree with this statement? Give your reasons.*

Although no official figures exist for homelessness amongst the young, one group, Centrepoint, estimates the number at over 50,000 16 to 19 year-olds in London alone. Since the mid 1980s the numbers of young homeless show an increase every year. Many young people face an impossible situation. They have no job so they cannot afford a home, and without a home address they cannot find a job. The obvious solution is to return home, but for many this is not an option.

Solving homelessness?

The 1960s saw public concern about the homeless growing especially after the showing of the film *Cathy Come Home* in 1966. This highlighted the plight of the homeless. There was a massive response to the programme and as a result, Shelter (The National Campaign for the Homeless) was set up.

Several other agencies exist to help the homeless. Every December Crisis at Christmas serves hot meals to the homeless as well as housing over 500 people every night. St Mungo's provides accommodation for over 1,000 people every night of the year in London. Centrepoint (the London based night shelter for young people) and the Salvation Army, provide hostels. There are housing charities such as The Peabody Trust which provides accommodation in London at affordable rates.

Activity

1 Role-play two scenes: one where two teenagers plan to run away together to a big city and discuss what they are going to do, where they are going to live and how much fun it will be. In the second role play, the couple three months later are living on the streets and facing lots of problems. Their dreams have gone as they now know what it is really like to be homeless.

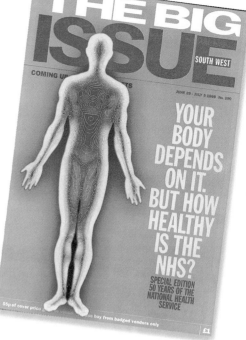

Crisis at Christmas and *The Big Issue*   **B**

Despite the efforts of these agencies some of the homeless get stuck in a vicious street cycle. Time and time again the same people move from the streets to hostels and then back to the streets. In 1991 an innovative campaign was launched through the publication and distribution of *The Big Issue*. This gave homeless people the ability to earn an income, to help themselves rather than rely on hand-outs. Many charities are very much about giving, whereas *The Big Issue* promotes self-help.

To become a vendor, a person must be vulnerably accommodated or homeless. All authorised vendors are trained and carry identification badges. They buy *The Big Issue* for a certain price and when they sell the magazine to the general public any profit they make they can keep.

All these organisations work towards the relief of the homeless and also help to keep the problem firmly in the public's view. Some also try to provide the means for people to become educated, trained and housed. Self-help is now seen as an essential part of the process and many charities try to put people in a better position to win control of their lives.

Activities

2 *The Big Issue* gives homeless people 'a hand-up and not a hand-out'. In pairs, discuss what you think this means.

3 Either, write a diary of a young homeless person, describing a day in their life or write a poem about life on the streets.

What do you think ?

The caption underneath this photo read: 'It could indeed be him, but last night it probably wasn't'. What point do you think is trying to be made? What do you feel when you look at the photo?

C   A homeless man and his dog in central London

Glossary

A

Aesthetic	Concerned with beauty or the appreciation of beauty. *98*
Anaemia	A deficiency in the red blood cells. *23*
Atrocities	Extremely cruel or wicked acts. *127*

B

'Back-street' abortion	The term given for an illegal abortion. *66*
Bias	Unfair or prejudiced. *76*
Buffer zone	An area situated between two countries which reduces the likelihood of hostility or war between them. *125*

C

Censored	Information suppressed by official authority on moral grounds. *56*
Chronic	Severe – persisting for a long time. *51*
Civil war	An internal war usually involving government forces fighting opposition from within their own country. *89*
Computer hacking	Accessing computer data without permission. *54*
Conception	The moment when a sperm fertilises an egg. *97*
Corrupt	Influenced by or using bribery or illegal activity. *125*
Cremation	A funeral ceremony during which the dead body is burned as opposed to buried. *112*

D

Deforestation	The complete clearance of forested land. *29*
Desertification	The turning of land, often through human mismanagement, into desert. *29*
Developed World	The richest countries in the world, normally found in the northern hemisphere. *61*
Developing World	Countries mainly in the southern hemisphere where the standard of living is far lower than that in the Developed World. *85*
Donors	Individuals who provide blood or an organ for transplantation. *95*

F

Fossil fuels	The term used to describe coal, oil and natural gas – fuels that have formed over millions of years and so are non-renewable. *79*

G

Genetic engineering	The process of changing the make up of living organisms. *39*
Genome	The complete genetic information about an organism. *39*
Great Depression	The term used to describe the economic collapse which occurred in the USA in 1929. It caused massive unemployment and widespread poverty throughout the rest of the world. *90*

H

Haemophiliac	A person suffering from a disease where the blood fails to clot normally. Even a slight injury can cause severe bleeding. *49*
Homicide	The killing of a human being by another person. *121*

I

Injunction	A court order instructing an individual not to commit a particular act. *56*
Innovative	To bring in change or use a new approach. *141*
Intravenous	Directly placed into a vein. *46*
In vitro fertilisation (test tube babies)	A method of treating infertility in which an egg is surgically removed from the ovary and fertilised in a laboratory. In vitro literally means 'in glass' and refers to the glass petri dish used in the process. *68*

K

Keyhole surgery	A less obtrusive method of surgery using the very latest medical technologies. *99*
Kibbutz	A form of communal living in Israel. *36*

L

Lasers	An acronym of light amplification by the stimulated emission of radiation – a device which produces an intense beam of light, infrared or ultraviolet radiation. *99*
Laxatives	Medication used to treat constipation. *12*
Leukaemia	Can be a fatal cancerous disease where too many leucocytes (white corpuscles) are accumulated in the body. *82*
Libelled	When a person's reputation is damaged by a written statement containing false information. *56*

M

Molotov cocktail(s)	Home-made incendiary 'bomb' usually consisting of a bottle filled with an inflammable liquid such as petrol. *104*
Morbid	An 'unhealthy' attitude with regard to death and dying. *110*

N

Norm	The usual or normal standard. *13*
Notoriety	Behaviour which is regarded as shameful or scandalous. *17*

P

Paradox	Puzzling – an absurd or contradictory statement. *113*
Parka(s)	A windproof jacket with a hood. *135*
Patent(s)	A government authority to an individual organisation ensuring the sole right to make or use or sell some invention. *42*
Patronised	Being treated as inferior, being 'put down'. *87*
Persecution	Unfair treatment normally on the grounds of political or religious belief. *100*
Plight	A problematic situation. *139*
Posthumous	Occurring after death. *62*
Psychologist	An individual who studies the human mind. *73*

R

Refugee	A person who has lost their home normally because of a war or natural disaster. *125*
Reincarnation	The belief in the rebirth of the spirit/soul in a new body. *113*
Role model(s)	A person looked to by others as an example. *121*

S

Sanctity	Sacred – something that is rare and precious and is to be valued. *64*
Sordid	Dirty or shabby. *129*
Sovereign	Supreme ruler or monarch. *126*
Stalking	To pursue or follow someone in an obsessive way. *72*
Stereotypes	Over-simplified or exaggerated pictures of people or situations. *76*
Stigma	A sign of disgrace or discredit. *49*

T

Therapy	The treatment of a disease or a physical/mental condition. *9*
Transgenic	An animal/plant having genetic material introduced from another species. *42*
Traumatic	Distressing or disturbing. *111*

W

Waif-like	Looking like a homeless/neglected child. *11*
Welfare State	A State system which provides support for the health and well being of all those in need. *90*